The Bishop's Cross

The Bishop's Cross

A Journey to the Truth

Wendy Hoke

eWriterUSA

Copyright © 2022 Wendy Hoke

Published by eWriterUSA

Cover Design by Wendy Hoke

No part of this book may be reproduced except in brief quotations
and in reviews without written permission from the publisher.

10 9 8 7 6 5 4 3 2 1

The Bishop's Cross
(Originally entitled *Family Legends, Family Lies*)
2022, Wendy Hoke

EWriterUSA.com

CONTENTS

CHAPTER v
DEDICATION ix
INTRODUCTION xi

1 | The Rules of Mountaineering | 1

2 | Sola Fide | 10

3 | Trekking in Nepal | 20

4 | Come Back, Love | 33

5 | Sexual Harassment | 38

6 | Puppets and Puppeteers | 43

7 | Life on La Cresta Drive | 51

8 | My Ally of Oriflamme Canyone | 60

9 | Mammoth Men I've Known - January 2022 | 68

CONTENTS

10	Valentine's Day on Villager Peak - February 2002	80
11	Easter at Gretchen's - March 31, 2002	86
12	Climbing Snow Creek - April 2002	94
13	Canon Tajo – Summer 2002	101
14	East to West – July 2002	106
15	Indian Head Peak	122
16	Tell Us, Danielle- August 2002	126
17	My Dream Mountain	134
18	Mother's Day at the Ritz Carlton	137
19	The Gay Priest	144
20	Epilogue	150
	ACKNOWLEDGEMENTS	159
	ABOUT THE AUTHOR	161

DEDICATION

Dedication

This book is dedicated to my charming, cheerful son, McKinley Armstrong Hoke, the greatest gift I ever received.

INTRODUCTION

Trekking in Nepal. Climbing Snow Creek. Camping in Anza Borrego. Mountain climbing and hiking in the High Sierras. Horseback riding and rock climbing in Canon Tajo. Stunning mountain top vistas, unexpected storms, gold mines, and icy alpine lakes are the backdrop.

This is an adventure in addition to a journey to the truth. After a stint on Wall Street, I made a change in life, joined Main Street, and took up mountain climbing. Along the way, I encountered rhinos, crocodiles, monkeys, elephants, tigers, bears, and a pack of Wild Englishmen.

What lessons did I learn in my real-life adventures? Speaking truth leads to a clear pathway that truth wins. Truth brings peace. Truth brings power. Truth brings light. Truth is light.

The commitment to truth, even when someone else works unendingly to keep secrets, is worth every struggle on that pathway.

The truth that needed to be spoken is this: my grandfather was a Bishop in the American Lutheran Church, and he was a pedophile who preyed on little girls in his own family, including me. He was a child molester, a rapist.

This journey examines the secrecy that surrounds this timely issue. Rather than graphic descriptions about the child sexual abuse (although you will understand what my grandfather did), I hope to enlighten the reader about how families keep these heinous acts

INTRODUCTION

secret. I also hope to convey some of the lasting emotional damage that sexual abuse of a child can cause.

My message is to find inner strength by speaking truth. My story speaks to the destructive cycle of fear and shame and how truth, compassion, mercy, and grace bring about peace of mind.

Those who have experienced CSA may want others to understand the family dynamics that enable a pedophile to continue to commit such acts. Family members need to understand the power that silence and shame can have over victims.

Until The Boston Globe broke the sex abuse scandal involving pedophile priests in the Catholic Church in 2002, no one would have believed that an ordained man of the church would commit such heinous crimes. Nor would anyone have believed that church hierarchy would cover up the crimes and transfer the molesters around, enabling them to continue damaging thousands of children.

It can be equally difficult to believe that a man would molest children within his own family. I believe that they hold a distinctive influence over those who might be inclined to speak up. As a society, we need to recognize this influence and work together to stop the harm inflicted on our girls and boys.

1

The Rules of Mountaineering

At some point in my life, I began climbing mountains. I don't recall the origin of this inclination. When I was a child, my family had a vacation home at Lake Arrowhead in the San Bernardino Mountains in Southern California. Yet, we were the type of family that strolled on tranquil mountain footpaths only when the comforts of enjoying hot cocoa by a large roaring fire beckoned in the evening. Nor do I have any recollection of camping with my parents, or even that they owned a tent.

My only experience as a child with camping came when I was about nine years old, maybe younger. My aunt and uncle took my brother and me to Mount Whitney in the Eastern Sierras where we hiked to the first lake. Perhaps that trip provided the impetus later in my life to head off to the Sierras whenever possible for the beauty and solitude.

Mountaineering differs from hiking. The term mountaineering describes a wide variety of activities related to climbing mountains. At one end of the spectrum, mountaineering can include peak bagging, for which little or no technical skills or equipment are necessary to reach the summit of a mountain. The other end of the spectrum includes full-blown expeditions to the highest peaks and the worst weather conditions on Earth. Some hikers consider themselves to be mountaineers. They are not. In truth, I am at best a peak bagger since I haven't climbed any of the truly big mountains of the world.

A mythical, all-inclusive set of mountaineering rules does not exist. However, over the years, I have discovered that each individual mountaineer tends to develop his or her own set of rules. Some are philosophical, frequently with a humorous bent such as: climb with passion; it's always taller than it looks; talk is cheap; no guts, no glory; and expect dead ends. Some rules speak to ethical behavior as a mountaineer: pack out more than you pack in; don't leave anyone behind; and render assistance to anyone who needs it regardless of the risk.

And some rules pertain to the practical aspects a mountaineer should focus on: if you are caught in a storm while in your tent, wait it out; don't take unnecessary risks; use the correct gear for the situation; buy the best gear you can afford.

The rule of mountaineering that I ascribe to is this:

1. Check your gear.
2. Double check your gear.
3. Triple check your gear.

A climber experiences increasing difficulty as the elevation rises. With each step, breathing becomes more labored, and the heart races almost uncontrollably due to the decreasing amount of oxygen available. Headaches, nausea, and dizziness sometimes occur.

To me, the view from the top is always worth the effort. However, each mountaineer has his or her own reason for climbing to the summit. The most famous reason came from George Leigh Mallory in 1923. When asked why he wanted to climb Mount Everest, Mallory retorted, "Because it's there!"

Non-mountain climbers do not realize that reaching the peak is only half the trip. Once at the top, a climber can briefly enjoy the view, but then must descend. Depending on the peak, getting down from the top can be as difficult, if not more so, than the climb up. More people die on descents than on ascents.

However, climbing the smaller peaks, while challenging, is rarely as dangerous as the ascent of a giant mountain. Still, I am the only person in my family that embraced the adventure. My parents adopted me as a newborn infant, so I sometimes wonder if it's genetic. I imagine my biological family carries some adventure gene that prompts them to seek out the higher altitudes despite the hard work just for the view from the top.

My adoptive family was a typical Southern California, middle class family as I was growing up in the 60s and 70s. We lived in a tiny college town east of downtown Los Angeles called Claremont. My father, Ritch Whitaker, was a mechanical engineer. As many engineers in Southern California, he worked on various aspects of NASA's race to the moon. He designed cryogenic valves and actuators used in the fuel systems of the Mercury, Gemini, and Apollo missions. Later, he designed components for super tankers that ship liquified natural gas. He was logical, rational, kind, and he had a quiet, wickedly funny sense of humor that would sneak up on you. His health was fragile due to type 1 diabetes and chronic bronchitis, but I can't recall any moment that he ever complained about how he felt physically.

Like many fathers, he enjoyed reading the sports page over breakfast. However, he would first pull out the Radio Shack ads to track the declining prices and shrinking sizes of the first Texas Instruments handheld calculators. He could barely contain his excitement when

Texas Instruments released the very first handheld calculator with a sine/cosine function. As an engineer who had knowledge of the technology developed through the space race, he would occasionally opine, "You know, someday cars will drive themselves." The technology existed in the 60s and 70s, but viable, affordable consumer applications were decades away. He would say these things, and I would think, "My dad is so smart, he knows the future."

My mother, Gretchen, graduated high school and attended a teaching hospital to attain her R.N. She worked hard to help put her husband through college, but after adopting children, she stayed home until my brother and I were in kindergarten. Later, she became a successful business woman and owned her own fabric stores. She was gregarious and well-liked by many. She was a gracious hostess who frequently opened her home to many family get-togethers at the holidays.

Her home was always decorated with impeccable taste, and she kept everything spotless despite two children and owning her own business. She was an excellent cook, skilled at sewing and homemaking, and she enjoyed collecting unique dishware and serveware that she used for her parties. Her taste in home furnishings was always perfect.

She and my dad met as teenagers at a Luther League beach party —Luther League being the Lutheran Church youth group. She was 14 and he was 17. I don't recall if the family stories relate that it was love at first sight. However, the family legends do relate that Ritch asked her what her father did for a living, so I always assumed that he had an eye for her. She told him, "He's a Lutheran pastor." Then she asked him the same. His response was classic for Ritch. He said, "My dad's a rabbi."

Gretchen didn't know what a rabbi was, so the joke was lost on her. After he asked her on a date, she asked her parents for permission to go. Of course, they wanted to know about him, including what his father did for a living. Gretchen responded, "Oh, he's a rabbi."

Family legends tend to become exaggerated over time, especially for the effect of humor. The version I heard as a child included Gretchen's parents retreating to the bedroom, and yelling could be heard coming from within.

This was 1950 in America and post WWII. Both of Gretchen's parents were of German descent—first generation in America—and the native tongue was occasionally spoken at home. It was most likely just as shocking for a German American pastor to hear that his daughter wanted to date the son of a rabbi as it was the other way around; the son of a rabbi wanted to date a second-generation German girl.

Eventually, the truth came out. My paternal grandparents were of English descent, Methodist, and Ritch's father was an all-American Ford dealer. When Ritch proposed to Gretchen, he told her, "I'll always be rich," a play on his name. They married when he was 22 and she was 19.

At some point, they discovered they couldn't have children. About six years into their marriage, they looked into adopting children. They adopted my brother first and two years later, I came home to them.

My parents ascribed to the "children should be seen and not heard" rule of rearing children, which was typical for many parents of the time. No one discussed emotions. Conversations remained exceedingly polite even when discussing hot topics such as politics. Among the adults, opinions were respected. However, the adults expected excellent behavior and no complaining from the children. In fact, complaining was frowned upon in general. "To complain is to put a burden on others" was a phrase I heard frequently. As ill as my father was, despite the years of pain, I never heard a gripe or a single mention about suffering or discomfort.

As parents, my mom and dad presented a united front to the children. I never witnessed any disagreement between them. My mother deferred to my dad. If she had other thoughts, she would save them for behind closed doors.

However, as a couple, my parents seemed truly happy, and Gretchen loved to prank Ritch. He graduated from USC, and the annual football game between USC and its cross-town rival, UCLA, was an exciting event. One year, my dad invited his USC friends to join us at the cabin in Lake Arrowhead for a weekend of USC festivities including watching the big game. Just as the men sat down in front of the TV to watch the lineups, my mother disappeared. As the players ran out from the locker rooms onto the playing field, my mother charged down the stairs into the living room dressed in a UCLA blue pleated skirt and yellow sweater while cheering for UCLA and waving blue and gold pom poms. My dad was so shocked, he spilled his coffee on his lap.

Several years later, we were seated at dinner. She had served corn as the vegetable, which was my dad's favorite. Every time we had corn, he would finish his entire meal. Then he would ask Gretchen if there was any more corn. She always had more made for him. However, one time she must have been tired of being asked.

So, on this particular night, she waited for him to ask, "Is there any more corn?"

"Yes, honey, of course there is. I'll get it for you," she replied.

Instead of taking his plate to dish corn onto it from the pot, she brought the pot to the table and poured its contents onto his empty dish. The result was a mountain of corn that barely stayed on the plate. There was a moment of silence before they broke into laughter.

When I was in high school, she began to take vacations to many different areas of the world. Up until that point, my father would occasionally join on a short trip, but his health didn't allow for much travel. Soon, Gretchen began going on her own with my dad's encouragement.

As far back as I can remember, my relationship with Gretchen was never good. I felt that she never seemed satisfied with me, and this feeling escalated as I became a teenager. Not being the cheerleader type as she had been, I tended more towards introversion and reading quietly in the library. I earned good grades and focused on academics. I thought it was this personality difference that caused the friction between us until many years later.

However, there were key events that solidified my feelings of inadequacy as her daughter. For my 16th birthday, she sat me down to tell me exciting news. She had a very special birthday present for me, and she knew that I would be so grateful. She had booked an appointment with a plastic surgeon for me to have rhinoplasty, a nose job.

After her lengthy lead-in about this magnificent gift that was going to be so expensive (but she would sacrifice for my benefit), she asked me, "Aren't you just thrilled?"

I was not thrilled. Rather, I was offended by the affront. Backtalk or impudence would be punished, and by that time after years of abuse, I had become very quiet and withdrawn. In addition, discourse with Gretchen was a futile endeavor. She dominated conversations when she wanted her way. She clearly wanted her way with the offensive "gift." She couldn't see beyond her own desires to observe the effect the offer had on me. I couldn't speak for myself at that point as that capability had been robbed from me long ago. With great reluctance, but polite thanks, I agreed to go to the appointment.

During the initial consultation, my mother and the surgeon spoke to each other and referred to me in the third person. He explained the procedure and offered several options.

Then my mother asked, "Which one will make her cute?"

The surgeon shot back at her, "She's already cute."

I remained silent through the entire appointment. But once home, I told my mother that I had changed my mind.

"But it's a gift. You should be grateful. I didn't raise you to be ungrateful."

I didn't budge, which was a rare moment for me. Typically, I simply gave in to her. But not this time. I thought I was cute enough, and she should have thought so too. To Gretchen, I was supposed to be filled with appreciation and thankfulness for her thoughtful present even though I had never expressed any concerns about my nose. I learned early on that Gretchen seemed incapable of understanding that she delivered insults wrapped as gifts.

Several years later in my early 20s, I came home for a formal dinner. I arrived before the other guests, and Gretchen greeted me at the door. As I stood in the entryway, she told me to wait a minute. She had been on a diet, although she was always slender. She came back with the bathroom scale, and she put it down in front of me.

"Let's compare. Who weighs less?" she said.

"I'm two inches taller than you. It would be comparing apples to oranges," I responded.

"Come on, just step on and we'll see who weighs less," she pushed.

"Why? Is it a competition?" I asked.

She had no response as I stood there waiting for her answer. She shrugged her shoulders and took the scale back to the bathroom.

My brother arrived with his girlfriend, Lynne, and they announced their engagement at dinner. I didn't know Lynne well, but

I was happy for the couple. However, as we were all saying our farewells after dinner, Gretchen hugged Lynne and said, "You're the daughter I've always wanted!" I was standing right there but said nothing, although I was deeply wounded.

My relationship with Gretchen, always shaky at best, took a deep dive with that comment. I began to stay away and attend only major holidays afterwards. Gretchen never questioned why or tried to invite me home more often. That was a very loud silent message. I wasn't pretty enough or outgoing enough for her. I felt as if she had written me off as her daughter—rejected and ignored.

Both of my parents were devoted Christians, and they taught me to count my blessings rather than focus on less than perfect circumstances. I was to thank God for the good things I had even in challenging times. Indeed, this practice of thanking God during difficulties and unpleasant moments is a tenet of Christianity as the Apostle Paul exhorted to the early church at Thessalonica in his first letter to them:

"Rejoice always, pray continually, give thanks in all circumstances; for this is God's will for you in Christ Jesus." 1 Thessalonians 5:18

Be grateful, appreciative, thankful, and always respectful towards the adults in the family. Regardless of how my mother treated you, impudence or complaining about anything was strictly verboten.

2

Sola Fide

My maternal grandfather, Konrad Frederick Koosmann, lived in Covina, California, which is a suburb of Los Angeles only about 20 miles west of Claremont. My maternal grandmother, Alice Koosmann, née Kolpack, passed away suddenly and unexpectedly when I was nine years old. I recall very little about her, only that I liked her, and she kept chocolate-covered ice cream bonbons in the freezer for the grandkids. At the time of her death, I felt sad. Still, I had no comprehension of the enduring legacy she left until much later in my life.

Konrad was an ordained pastor of the American Lutheran Church, which later merged with the Lutheran Church in America to form the current Evangelical Lutheran Church in America. He served as the Bishop of the Pacific Region (or District President as it was briefly called) for several terms before returning to pastoring a single church, Christ Lutheran Church on Citrus Street in Covina.

He grew up in rural Wisconsin deep in farm country, and he first worked as a schoolteacher before going off to seminary. He loved to tell stories about himself growing up, and typically they involved pranking others, which I assumed is where Gretchen learned to do the same.

I heard one story many times. As a teenager, he went out to begin working the frozen dirt in the vegetable garden as the winter snow had just melted in the early spring. He came upon a large, dead, frozen rat, and he thought the tail looked just like a weed. He dug a hole and buried the rat with the frozen tail sticking out of the hole. Then he ran into the house to his sister, Hilda.

"Hilda! Come quick! There's a huge weed in the vegetable garden, and I'm not strong enough to pull it out. Come help!" he told her.

Hilda went marching out, grabbed the weed/tail, and pulled her hardest. That frozen rat came flying out of the loosely packed dirt and hit her right in the face.

She was angry and going to tell on him. But he convinced her to put the rat back into the ground and do the same to the next sister, Frieda. Then Konrad convinced Frieda to get Elsa, and Elsa to get Erna. One by one they agreed, and the scene played out four times as he managed to get each of his four sisters hit in the face with a disgusting dead rat.

Konrad would laugh and laugh whenever he told that family legend. I never did understand the humor. Instead, I was always appalled by the story of humiliating his sisters.

He would tell another family legend about himself as well. One hot summer day, he demanded that his mother make him buckwheat pancakes for breakfast. She declined because she didn't want to stoke the wood-burning stove in the steaming hot weather. In a furious rage at his mother, he punched a hole in the wall of the kitchen behind the door.

"My father told me my punishment would be looking at the hole in the wall as we sat at the table to eat dinner. It was meant to make me feel guilty, but my mother should have made me what I wanted! Buckwheat pancakes! That was her job!"

Konrad held the position of patriarch in our family in the very traditional sense. He set the rules and tone of the family. He was venerated and respected without question. Since he was a pastor, religion also ruled and set the tone over the children and grandchildren. His parents had emigrated from eastern Germany (now Poland) to Canada, where he was born in 1908. They eventually moved south into Wisconsin. He met Alice Kolpack, also of German descent, and married her at the Lutheran Church in Bowler, Wisconsin. Prior to receiving his Doctoral of Divinity, he worked as a schoolteacher. Apparently, he heard the call of the west because he and his wife moved out to Los Angeles prior to 1936, the year my mother was born.

Konrad was the family's pastor as well. We attended his Lutheran church in Covina. My parents were married there as were her three siblings, and he officiated their ceremonies. He baptized me and my brother at that church. After he retired, we continued to attend that church until we moved south to Orange County.

Gretchen spoke very highly of her father, although I remember very little about her relationship with her own mother. My father and Konrad seemed very close to me. It has taken me many years of pondering their relationship to even come close to guessing why they were so close. When Ritch was in his late teens, he loved drag racing late at night against his friends. Indeed, this was a popular sport in the early 50s in Southern California. He had a friend who would race with him. One night, Ritch got out and let his friend race the next round alone. His buddy crashed the car and was killed. Several years later when he and Gretchen had been married for only two years, his father took his own life. Eventually, I surmised that perhaps Konrad filled a deep void and provided a father figure for Ritch. Most likely, Konrad assured him of God's love for him.

Family gathered for holiday celebrations on Christmas, Thanksgiving, and Easter. Christmas was always a favorite, as all joined together to observe the birth of Jesus. On Christmas Eve, we enjoyed a formal meal before heading to the living room to open presents and have dessert and coffee. Each year, Konrad would begin the festivities by first reading the Christmas story from the Gospel of Luke Chapter 2, which is the most detailed account of Christ's birth. Although only about 5' 6" tall, Konrad possessed a deep, baritone voice that made for some impressive preaching and Bible reading. His voice soared as he read the verses describing the Virgin Mary, the baby in the manger, the shepherds in the fields, and the multitude of heavenly angels singing praises to God.

On some occasions, my grandparents would watch my brother and me to give my parents a break. Konrad was quite the beer drinker, and he didn't try to hide it. Beer drinking came with the German background. Frequently I watched while he finished an entire six pack of Pabst in about an hour after working in his vegetable garden under the blistering summer sun. Once I reached the age of 7 or 8, he would pour a glass of beer and hand it to me with the words, "Good little German girls know how to drink beer." This was the prelude to the sexual abuse if I was alone with him.

As a Lutheran pastor, he preached on the chief principle of Lutheranism, which is Sola Fide, or justification by faith alone.

Martin Luther (1483 - 1546), the extremist monk who stood up to the corrupt Pope Leo X (1475 - 1521) and essentially launched the Lutheran church, represented the center of the church of my youth. We celebrated Reformation Day, the day Luther posted his 95 Theses on the door of Wittenberg Castle church in 1517 challenging the Catholic Church's corruption of the day. And, we memorized Luther's Small Catechism.

We believed in the foundation of Sola Fide, justification by faith alone through God's grace. Luther stood on this foundation in opposition to Leo, even as Leo excommunicated the monk for his heretical teachings in 1521.

You cannot earn your way into heaven through good works. This is the basis of Sola Fide. Indeed, good works in conjunction with faith cannot get you into heaven. Faith in Jesus Christ alone by the Grace of God does that.

From my perspective, life in my family meant focusing only on faith, frequently at the expense of other scriptures such as the epistle from James, the half-brother of Jesus, who addressed the issue of faith versus works this way:

"What good is it, my brothers and sisters, if someone claims to have faith but has no deeds? Can such faith save them? Suppose a brother or a sister is without clothes and daily food. If one of you says to them, "Go in peace; keep warm and well fed," but does nothing about their physical needs, what good is it? In the same way, faith by itself, if it is not accompanied by action, is dead." James 2: 13-17

The problem of faith versus good works has been debated for millennia. Over my life, I adopted a stance that faith without good works is more than dead. It is the embodiment of evil because a person of faith cannot inherently ignore good works.

Theologians may disagree with me, but this is how I recall being taught as a child: faith alone and acceptance of Jesus as Savior. Once accepting Christ, you get into heaven, although this gives many nonbelievers pause when they consider that the most heinous criminals could receive God's forgiveness if they accept Christ. An anecdote attributed to the Nuremberg Trial era illustrates this quandary.

A group of Jewish rabbis approached some Christian pastors. They asked:

"If Hitler on his deathbed accepted Jesus as his Savior, then he went to Heaven regardless of his deeds on earth. A righteous Jew who spent his life doing good works and worshipping the God of Abraham, Isaac, and Jacob, but thinks the Messiah is yet to come, that person went to hell. That is what you believe?"

After the Christians consulted with each other privately, they answered, "Yes, that is what we believe."

In my opinion, Sola Fide can lead to a slippery slope without the complementary tenets of confession and repentance. Humans in their depravity focus on their own faith rather than the object of that faith, which is God. They ignore their faults knowing that they already have entrance into heaven and eternal life. Then comes the bragging about their faith being greater than another's, the finger pointing, judging of others, the log in your own eye as you strive to pick out the speck in someone else's eye. "This person is a strong Christian and not that person," and so on.

Even worse, what if you have faith in the wrong thing? Your beliefs may be sincere, and all your fellow congregation members may deem you to be a "strong Christian," but what if that faith is not firmly in Jesus Christ? What will your works look like? This can happen in churches in which the pastor develops a cult following. Congregation members worship the pastor rather than God.

The way I see it is that faith saves, but good works cement your feet into the cornerstone of the foundation of God's church, that cornerstone being Christ. We're all human and make mistakes. Still, truly bad works without confession, repentance, and change betray the real heart.

The irony within the Lutheran church that I grew up in, with roots in the Midwestern Lutheran churches and members largely of German descent, is that the doctrine of Sola Fide applied only to men as a pragmatic matter.

In practice, the women in my Lutheran church experience worked very hard, in contrast to the message put forth in the Gospels. The prime example of this dichotomy was Mary and Martha who symbolized the tensions between faith and good works. They symbolized women's roles in the church.

For readers not familiar with the story, Mary and Martha were sisters and among the women who followed Jesus during his ministry. Their brother was Lazarus, whom Jesus raised from the dead. The Gospel of John records that Jesus loved the three siblings and is the only Gospel that tells of raising Lazarus. The Gospel of Luke records an encounter between Jesus and Martha that for millennia has been used to define women in the church.

"As Jesus and his disciples were on their way, he came to a village where a woman named Martha opened her home to him. She had a sister called Mary, who sat at the Lord's feet listening to what he said. But Martha was distracted by all the preparations that had to be made. She came to him and asked, 'Lord, don't you care that my sister has left me to do the work by myself? Tell her to help me!'

'Martha, Martha,' the Lord answered, 'you are worried and upset about many things, but few things are needed—or indeed only one. Mary has chosen what is better, and it will not be taken away from her.'" Luke 10: 38-42

Mary sat. Martha worked.

Poor Martha. Thousands of years later, she is remembered as a complainer and ignorant of the truly important things in life. All she tried to do was treat Jesus with the customary hospitality of her culture.

I've always believed that Martha got a bad rap. When Lazarus was sick, they sent for Jesus. Jesus intentionally waited two days before taking off for Bethany. As he arrived after Lazarus' death, it was Martha who went out to meet him, and she professed a deeper faith than Mary did.

In the Lutheran church, you were either a Mary or a Martha if you were female, although I knew far more Marthas than Marys in my childhood. The women cooked, served, and cleaned up. The men sat in the living room to chat with one another. Being a Mary was an ideal that was impractical to the social conventions.

If we take the story of Mary and Martha in which Martha complains as Mary sits, I interpret the scene as Christ toppling traditional gender roles. Mary took a place among the men to listen to Christ's teachings. In my opinion, he toppled gender roles with other encounters as well. At the very least, my interpretation is that he sought to give women equal footing. Somehow, the culture of ancient Israel and gender roles remained rigid in that area, or perhaps the male dominated priesthood chose to ignore certain teachings.

In 1992, Janet Letnes Martin published a satire that hysterically captured the Midwest Lutheran church culture. Entitled *Lutheran Church Basement Women,* the book spoofed the church institution that created the real phrase "basement women." Basement women were always Marthas, not Marys. They belonged to circles, which were named after women in the Bible like Martha Circle, Esther Circle, Ruth Circle, and on. However, only respectable women in the Bible had circles named for them. There was never a Delilah Circle, Job's Wife Circle, Woman Caught in Adultery Circle, or Woman at the Well Circle. Each circle cooked for a specific type of church gathering, from funerals and baptisms to weddings. In the Midwest, the churches had the kitchens in the basement. Hence, they became known by the insulting, degrading moniker "basement women."

Basement women knew the six types of aprons and owned extensive collections of each type of apron, carried wooden spoons in their apron pockets, and knew how to tie the right knots in dishtowels for serving hotdishes (not casseroles!). They wrote poetry about Jell-O, cooked dead spreads, called their desserts "bars," poured fancy Lutheran cocktails (tomato juice in a chilled glass), held firm beliefs on whether Hellmann's or Miracle Whip was the best mayonnaise, and passive-aggressively derided Marys. The book spawned a mini-cult following that inspired a musical comedy called "Lutheran Basement Ladies."

Basement women worked from sunup to sundown, mopping floors, washing windows, cleaning toilets, cooking meals, even washing walls. Gretchen would do that once a year. She would get a big bucket, ladder, and TSP. Then she would wash the inside walls from floor to ceiling.

"Well, in Germany, the women scrub the exterior walls too, "she would exclaim.

As a child, I did as the Marthas in my family directed me to do. However, I didn't grow up to be either a Mary or a Martha. I didn't fit in that way. The adventure gene in my DNA didn't allow for that scenario. Thus, I have taken comfort for many years in the fact that the Bible has many mountain climbers in it, even if they weren't women mountain climbers. Abraham climbed the mountain, as God directed, to sacrifice his son, Isaac (relieved of that task at the last moment thankfully). Moses climbed Mount Sinai to receive the Ten Commandments and Mount Abarim to see the Promised Land before dying. Elijah climbed Mount Carmel. King David wrote Psalm 121:

"I will lift up my eyes to the mountains,
Where does my strength come from?"

And of course, Jesus climbed Mount Tabor for the Transfiguration and the Mount of Olives to pray on the eve of his arrest.

So, even if no one else in my adoptive family climbed mountains and all the women were either Marys or Marthas, I always believed I had worthwhile role models just the same.

3

Trekking in Nepal

Through the late 80s and 90s in my early adulthood, I rarely returned home to visit my parents. I loved my father, but I simply could not tolerate being around Gretchen.

I moved to San Diego in 1989, and from there I took numerous camping and hiking trips around the western states. A multitude of outdoor activities are only a short drive from San Diego. Sometimes I went by myself for solitude, but mostly I had a wide circle of friends who also enjoyed the adventure and activities. However, I went on a trip with some unexpected fellow travelers that changed my life forever.

In September 1997, Gretchen, Lynne and I went trekking in Nepal. By that time, Lynne was divorced from my brother. Gretchen gave this trip as a Christmas gift to both Lynne and me. The trek was The Royal Trek, designed by the natives for a visit by Prince Charles. I was surprised by the gift. Gretchen frequently invited my younger cousins on her expeditions and paid for them. I never had an answer when other family members would ask why she took other people's children, but not her own.

Gretchen presented the gift of the trip to both Lynne and me as we sat in her living room. I had mixed feelings, but remained silent. I learned a long time ago that her gifts to me frequently came wrapped in ulterior motives. Finally, I was invited on a trip with my mother only to share it with Lynne, the daughter she always wanted.

Still, I agreed to go along on the trip to Nepal and did my best to seem thankful and grateful.

We flew into Katmandu and headed west to Pokhara. There we met up with the Sherpas, guides, and cooks who would escort us on our hike through the lower foothills of the Annapurna range of the Himalayas. The highest altitude we reached was no more than 6,000 ft, but we could see the big mountains from exquisite vantage points.

No written description or photographs can substitute for seeing those mountains in person. In California, the cloud cover obscures our picturesque Sierra Mountain range with its many 14,000 ft peaks. But the Himalayas rise above the cloud cover, and the alabaster peaks float in the heavens. When flying in Nepal, you look out the airplane window and up at the peaks. No one looks down on the Himalayan range.

This was a trip arranged by a tour company. Seven Americans made up our group: a young couple, two older sisters who were celebrating a reunion, and our three. One of the sisters was in her late 60s or early 70s, and the guide made sure she had two porters with her to help her along the trek.

The Royal Trek is a relatively short trek along the foothills of the Annapurna range and north of the Pokhara valley. The trek offers a delightful mix of experiencing the Nepalese people and culture in their villages as well as stunning vistas looking out at Machhapuchhre (Fishtail) peak, Annapurna I, Dhaulagiri, Manaslu, and Langtang.

We trekked through tiny hamlets where young Nepalese children would run out to greet us with their only English: "You like Coca-Cola?" We offered them trinkets such as stickers, pencils, crayons, and bubble gum. The Nepalese were so poor, but they all seemed to be completely happy and always smiling. "Namaste! Namaste!" Soon into the trek, we were out of range of any electricity or transportation beyond some bicycles.

The cooks prepared what they believed Americans like to eat, lots of eggs, meat, and toast. However, I was a strict vegetarian at that time, so I asked for what the porters were eating, rice and dal, which is lentil curry. We had been very careful about not drinking the local water to prevent illness, but the cooks made the rice with water right from the Karnali River. I hesitated a bit, since we had passed many Nepalese washing their clothes and their yaks in the river. Still, I ate like the locals ate, and I didn't get sick.

On one of the final nights before heading back to Katmandu, we camped on a plateau with adjacent huts belonging to the natives. The site had a stunning vista of the mountains. Our porters erected a large white tent and informed us that a celebratory dinner would be cooked and served inside. Outside the tent on one of the supporting poles hung several live chickens upside down by their legs, which we learned would become dinner.

As a group, we relaxed in a circle of chairs as we enjoyed afternoon tea. Jokes about the chickens going into the tent and not coming out alive began to fly. This prompted Gretchen to tell the group about a summer trip during which Konrad took the grandchildren to Wisconsin after Alice had passed away.

My brother and I were two of the grandchildren. I was 9, and he was 11. The other grandchildren were my three cousins from my father's side, so not really Konrad's grandchildren. They were 6, 10, and 13.

Konrad's sister and brother-in-law who lived in rural Wisconsin wanted to take a lengthy vacation. The brother-in-law was a Lutheran pastor for three very tiny rural churches, and Konrad agreed to cover for him by pastoring the churches while staying at their home in Tilleda, Wisconsin. It became known in our family as the legendary trip during which the city kids learned about farming and real life.

Gretchen spoke about how wonderful the trip was, and how Konrad had managed five children for over two months. He made us memorize a Bible verse every week, and he kept track of the food we ate. He logged how many bushels of potatoes and gallons of milk we consumed, and he told the parents how much he spent on food. They had contributed money towards the food for the kids. However, he went over budget, and this was his way of justifying the additional expenditures.

Each Sunday, we all went to the three churches for services. They were small congregations filled almost exclusively with farm families. On the first Sunday at the first church, he had all five of us children stand up in the pews during the service. He introduced us as the city kids. Then he suggested that any of the families could host some or all of the kids for a week, and he would pick us up the next Sunday.

It was a very bizarre suggestion: pass off the children onto total strangers. Still, it worked. At the first church, someone offered to take one or two of us during the week. Then we went on to the second and third church, where he repeated the performance. On Monday, Konrad drove us out to the homes for the week. Then he picked us up at church on the following Sunday. This scene repeated itself for several weeks over the summer. On more than one occasion, for some reason I was not picked up by a farm family and spent the week alone with Konrad back in Tilleda. He made sure I drank plenty of beer on those weeks alone with him.

The live chickens destined to be our dinner that night in Nepal reminded Gretchen of one lesson Konrad taught us on that summer trip to Wisconsin.

He purchased two live chickens from a local farmer. He was determined to teach the city kids where food really comes from. We were to slaughter, prepare, and eat the chickens for dinner that night. I seem to recall that my brother took the ax to the chickens' necks, although it may have been Konrad. The headless chickens took off in maniacal flight until their nervous systems ran out of steam and landed them as motionless lumps of feathers in the grass. Then we had to retrieve those headless lumps, pluck the feathers and gut them. Konrad had us line up the internal organs on newspaper and label them. We laid out the eggs in varying stages of development as well. There are still photos of that scene floating around in my family somewhere, and I can still hear Konrad's booming laughter at the gruesome sight.

As Gretchen relished regaling the group with the tale and praising her own father for teaching the citified kids such a valuable lesson, the younger sister on the reunion trip, Aileen, gave Gretchen a sharp rebuke.

"Gretchen, that's child abuse!" she said.

A moment of shock flashed across Gretchen's face, and a brief moment of silence followed as Gretchen sought to compose herself.

I took that brief moment of silence as an opportunity, and I loudly and firmly said, "Thank you."

The Nepalese porters and Sherpas stopped their work and stared at the group. They spoke no English, but they understood the tones of the voices.

Someone changed the subject, and soon we were called to supper in the tent with our celebratory chicken dinner.

The direction of my life changed that evening. Aileen opened the door to finally addressing the abuse with Gretchen. Aileen had never met Konrad, but she knew child abuse when she heard it, and she called it for what it was. I had never heard anything so truthful about him before. That night was the first time I began to realize that I could in fact talk about the sexual abuse. How to talk about it was a dilemma. But in retrospect, that was the day I began to take back my own narrative— a narrative that had been dominated by Konrad and Gretchen.

Very late that night, pained groaning came from one of the tents. The groans turned to cries of severe pain, and the entire camp awoke. Sherpas and porters were moving about as the older sister, Helen, became very ill. Gretchen and Aileen tried to assist, but this situation became very serious, very quickly.

We were in the outback. There was no 911 or cell phones. There were no landlines either. In fact, no transportation existed nearby. A porter left in the wee hours of the morning to hike down the mountain to the first village with a bus. The bus took him to the first village with a phone. From there, he called the rescue helicopter, but it had just left to pick up a climber with a broken leg in the Everest region. The helicopter arrived at our camp around 3:00 p.m. to pick up Helen and evacuate her and Aileen to Katmandu. She died from peritonitis during the helicopter ride.

The group moved on with just five of us that morning. We trekked out back towards Pokhara not knowing Helen's fate. A day or two later when we met up with our group leader in Pokhara, he informed us of her death. He made a short, somewhat curt announcement, although this may have been a cultural way of dealing with death or his limited English. We were all stunned. The others were shocked that this could happen, although I had hiked in the outback long enough to know that you take risks. I also considered the randomness that we were all on the same trek. We knew each other for only five days, yet Aileen changed my life forever. I doubt she ever had a clue that her words had so much impact.

After finishing the Royal Trek, the three of us broke off on our own. We took a separate jaunt to southwestern Nepal to visit two national parks that border India, Chitwan and Bardia. Our guide took us to the Katmandu airport, gave us box lunches, and the following instructions:

"When you arrive at Nepalgunj Airport, a porter from Chitwan will meet you and take your luggage, your tickets, and passports for safekeeping. You will be fine."

Upon arrival at Nepalgunj Airport, we disembarked from our ten-seat puddle jumper onto a short tarmac. Hundreds of military soldiers carrying machine guns surrounded the airport. The pilot directed us to the only building within sight. Inside I could see essentially two main rooms, one of which appeared to be a customs-type check, and the other for baggage claim.

I made my way to the baggage claim area to meet up with Gretchen and Lynne. It was a small room, dank, dirty, and with only one bare light bulb hanging from the ceiling.

The baggage started to come through the chute. Before we could move towards our luggage, a man darted through the crowd, grabbed all of it in his hands and ran off. He disappeared completely. I was stunned.

"Well," Lynne said, "maybe that's the guy from Chitwan."

We stood in the small room for several hours. We were all alone, the only women in sight, and had no way to communicate with those around us. The baggage claim area began to empty except for the soldiers with their machine guns.

Suddenly, a Nepalese man came running up to us. He was totally toothless and was waving his arms maniacally. He could not speak, but kept frantically motioning, not pointing go here, go there. His arms were like windmills. Lynne handed him our tickets and passports. Then he disappeared.

So, there we were. We had no luggage, tickets, or passports. We were halfway around the world from home and surrounded by heavily armed military.

Dusk fell quickly, and we went outside to the curb. We sat down on a brick wall, and halfheartedly picked at the food in our box lunches. Then we stood up and meandered to the other side of the street.

No one wanted to express the rising fear we each felt. We remained quiet waiting for each other to speak. I was silently upset with Lynne for handing our tickets and passports to a stranger.

"Are you going to Chitwan?" a male voice with a British accent asked us.

"I believe this is your truck. I'll be riding with you part of the way. I'm going to Bardia, but my truck is behind schedule. So, I will go with you until they catch up."

We turned to see a man, quite handsome, in his early to mid 40s dressed in trekking gear. A Jeep with an open truck bed was at the curb.

"You are the American ladies, are you not? Going to Chitwan? This is your ride."

After some hesitation, we got into the open Jeep bed, as did the English gentleman, and our Jeep took off into the pitch-dark night.

"I'm sorry to hear about your trekking companion," the man said. "How unfortunate that she passed away before making it back to Katmandu. My sincere condolences, and I hope that the rest of your trip goes well, despite the setback."

I was a bit surprised. How did this man know about that?

"By the way, let me introduce myself," he continued. "My name is John Havens. I'm with Oxventure out of Oxford, England. I come here to Nepal twice a year to lead expeditions. Our goal is to take groups of people, some with disabilities and some without disabilities, and take them to the summit of Kala Pattar to see Mount Everest. We have even taken a man in a wheelchair to the top of Kala Pattar."

"How did you ever decide to do something like this?" Gretchen asked him.

"Well, I lead scientific expeditions all over the world. And I make gobs and gobs of money doing what I love to do. So, this is my way of giving something back. Besides, I love this country and the people. They are so warm-hearted."

"You ladies are from the U.S.? I once went to a lovely place called Sisters, Oregon. I met a nice woman, who invited me to sit in a hot tub and look out over the scenery, the mountains..."

"That was a scientific expedition?" I asked.

He smiled. "Yes, scientific."

Headlights were approaching quickly from behind. John said something to the driver. The Jeep stopped, and John hopped out.

"This is my truck to Bardia. They finally caught up. Don't worry about anything. They will take very good care of you at Chitwan. Perhaps we will meet up again."

Then our jeep took off again into the black night.

The staff at Chitwan did indeed take good care of us. Our luggage was in our rooms, and the staff informed us that our tickets and passports were locked in the safe in the office. The two crazy men at the airport were employees of the parks.

We spent three days at Chitwan enjoying the elephant rides searching for tigers. We took day hikes and encountered rhinos on the trails. Hundreds of Rhesus monkeys played in the trees, and crocodiles hovered in the water at the river's edge.

The excursion should have been a peaceful encounter with nature. Certainly, the staff quietly worked to ensure that each guest was comfortable in the hotel. The environment of the surrounding park encouraged calm and serenity amid the verdant landscape.

However, my irritation with Gretchen was growing. Not only was my irritation piqued when I had the realization that I could finally call Konrad an abuser, I also tried and failed to ignore a new habit Gretchen demonstrated repeatedly while on the trip. When meeting someone new, she would introduce Lynne first as her daughter. Then pointing to me, she would say, "That's my other daughter, Wendy." She did this repeatedly with our group of seven during the Royal Trek, and Lynne did nothing to correct her. Throughout the entire trip, Gretchen and Lynne hung out together and rarely included me. In a very real way, I was alone on the trek.

My brother and Lynne had been divorced for years, and this new practice of Gretchen's was acutely painful to me. Gretchen's pronouncement at their engagement that Lynne was the daughter she always wanted left a deep emotional bruise in me. That bruise began to grow and rip open on this trip. Still, I remained silent out of habit until one night.

While at dinner on one of our last nights at Chitwan, Gretchen did it again. She introduced Lynne as her daughter to another visitor and then pointed at me as an afterthought. Once again, Lynne did nothing to correct Gretchen.

I could no longer endure the outrage. I abruptly stood up and left the dining room without saying why. I went back to the hotel room that Lynne and I were sharing. Gretchen had her own private room.

A few moments later, Gretchen knocked on the door and came in. She wanted to know what was wrong.

"She's not your daughter. Lynne is not your daughter. She is your former daughter-in-law. I am your daughter. I remember what you told her at their engagement dinner, about being the daughter you always wanted. It's cruel."

Gretchen's response was classic for her. She assumed what I long before dubbed the "Koosmann Stance," which was a way of standing with her left hand resting on the backside of her hip, palm upward. Konrad frequently stood that way, although with his right hand, not left.

Then she blamed me.

"You misunderstood. I was just trying to simplify things. It's easier to introduce Lynne as my daughter than try to explain that she and David are divorced."

My indignation grew into outright resentment and vexation. I was close to tears, but I would not let her see it.

"No one cares if Lynne is divorced from David. No one here knows them, and after we return, you will never see these people again. What does it take to be accepted in this family? I remember what you said. Do you ever stop to consider how painful that is to me, especially since I'm adopted?

"It has nothing to do with you being adopted," Gretchen said. "I simply introduced Lynne as my daughter to make it easy."

"Easy? It's about you then? Yes, it's always about you and your pretenses, never how anyone else feels."

I was angry and hurt. Aileen's comment about Konrad's child abuse fueled my passion at that moment. I saw an opening to finally address the abuse with the person who should have protected me. I was in my mid-30s at the time, yet it was the first time I ever heard anyone say something so truthful about Konrad. Criticism of Konrad was not allowed and always punished if it did happen. At that moment, I hadn't considered whether Gretchen might be a victim as well. I only knew that I had been horribly physically and emotionally abused.

All the enmity, hostility, and anger came flooding forth, and I flung my accusations at her.

"It is about being adopted. Do you know what your father said to me once? He said, 'I don't approve of adopted children. They are defective, there's always something wrong with them.' Seriously, do you stop to think how emotionally abusive that is?"

Gretchen's face flinched just a bit. But she also doubled down on the Koosmann Stance. She wore a facial expression of dismissive self-righteousness, a self-certainty meant to shut the other person down immediately. I could tell she had heard Konrad express his disdain for adopted children before, most likely when she and my father adopted my brother. She likely heard it again two years after that when they adopted me.

"I don't believe he said that. Again, you misunderstood. Of course, you're accepted in this family," she said.

"Of course, he said it. I didn't make it up. You heard Aileen, he committed child abuse. She heard it right away. She knew it and called it by its true name. It's child abuse. Your father was an abuser. And calling adopted children defective is just the excuse he used to blame the victim and deflect any attention to what he did."

Deep down, I knew that this was not how I wanted to broach the subject of sexual abuse, but I at least wanted to open the door that Konrad was an abuser. In retrospect, this was not the time, way, or place I had planned on. But Aileen had thrown the door wide open, and I ran right through that door at break-neck speed.

"How dare you say that about my father! He is a great, loving man; he is a man of God," Gretchen announced. Then she turned around and left the room in defiance.

Eventually, Lynne came back to the room. We said nothing to one another that night. The rest of the trip was extremely unpleasant to me. Gretchen and Lynne were inseparable throughout the last days, frequently doing things together as a pair while I was left alone.

4

Come Back, Love

We saw John Havens the next day. We were relaxing at the bar area of Bardia after transferring there in the morning from Chitwan and enjoying our afternoon tea. John was there.

He greeted the three of us, and he sat down next to me. He asked how our trip had been thus far, and he explained that his group would be arriving soon. They were rafting down the Karnali River.

"I like to play a little joke on them," he said. "When they arrive at the pier, the guide tells them Bardia is a hike of about several kilometers. Everyone will rearrange their gear and repack it for the hike. But really it's only about 50 meters."

We chatted about the trip, and then we heard voices coming from the river. His group had arrived, and he excused himself to greet his travelers.

We left to take afternoon showers, hoping the sun had warmed the water enough by then. Then we relaxed while overlooking the Karnali until dinner.

After dinner we went back to the bar area for tea. John and his group were there enjoying the sunset and view.

I was reading *Angela's Ashes* by Frank McCourt, and I had almost finished it. Gretchen and Lynne had their own books. John came over and sat down next to me.

"I read that book last year," he said. "It's quite a sad story."

"Yes, sad," I replied. "But I have a rather quirky sense of humor. This poor mother keeps having babies, and they keep dying. Then she has more babies. At some point in the book, it reminded me of the musical skit from Monty Python's The Meaning of Life."

John paused and then the connection came to him. He started laughing and started to sing the theme song of the skit but caught himself. ("Every sperm is sacred, every sperm is great. If one sperm gets wasted, God gets quite irate!")

"I love Monty Python," I said. "I can quote the entire scripts from The Meaning of Life and The Holy Grail. And in my opinion, Life of Brian is the best documentary ever filmed."

He was laughing harder.

"Cheer up, Brian. You know what they say: some things in life are bad. They can really make you mad. Other things just make you swear and curse. When you're chewing on life's gristle, don't grumble; give a whistle, and this'll help things turn out for the best. And... always look on the bright side of life..."

"Or, my personal favorite," I continued, "Listen. Strange women lying in ponds distributing swords is no basis for a system of government. Supreme executive power derives from a mandate from the masses, not from some farcical aquatic ceremony. Well, but you can't expect to wield supreme executive power just 'cause some watery tart threw a sword at you! I mean, if I went 'round saying I was an emperor just because some moistened bint had lobbed a scimitar at me, they'd put me away!"

"I have never met anyone, certainly not an American, who could quote Monty Python better than I could!" John said.

There was definitely an instant connection between us, and I wanted to pursue it. But just then, my mother got curious about the laughter and came over to join in. She began dominating the conversation. John was polite to her, but I was upset. I was still very angry with Gretchen for her insensitivity. But I couldn't be impolite to my mother in front of other people, nor could I think of a way to give her a hint to go away.

Lynn announced she was going to bed, and I followed her. Gretchen followed as well. Back at the room we were sharing, I convinced Lynne that we should go back out to socialize.

She agreed and we went back out. John was sitting with his group and invited us to join in. I told a story about an encounter with a merchant in Kathmandu. The incident had both Gretchen and Lynne in stitches, but the humor of it was lost on the British group.

Lynne and I got up to leave, and John said, "No, stay, a while longer!"

We excused ourselves, and I could hear John saying, "Wendy, come back!"

The next morning, I inquired about John and his group with the staff. They informed me that his group had left early in the morning. I thought I would never see him again. At the bar area was a guest book to sign one's name, address, phone number, and animals sighted. I filled it out, and for animals sighted I wrote: "Rocky, Bullwinkle, and a pack of wild Englishmen."

We were to take a Jeep back to Nepalgunj airport for a flight back to Katmandu. While waiting for the ride out, I went out to the patio area for tea and sat down by myself. I was alone, and the peaceful sounds of the park were almost hypnotic.

A man approached and sat down next to me. The sun was in my eyes, and it took me a moment to realize the man was John Havens. He hadn't left yet.

We talked for about twenty minutes. He wanted to know all about me, and I, him. But the inevitable happened. My mother came out from her tent and sat down next to him and began dominating the conversation once again with talk about herself. She talked about her safaris in Kenya, her trips to Egypt, the Holy Land, and everywhere else. She was oblivious to the fact that John was interested in me, certainly not her.

Again, John was polite, and I was upset. I said I had to get out of the sun, and I went into the bar.

A few moments later the Jeep arrived. I got up to leave just as John was coming into the bar. He approached me and put out his hand. I put out my hand to meet his, and he held my hand between both of his. He did not let go. We looked at each other without saying anything. Then I slowly pulled my hand away and wished him well.

On the flight between Delhi and London, my mother began talking about John and how wonderful and delightful he was. I snapped. I was extremely rude to my mother.

"Do you really think he sat down next to me just to hear you talk about yourself? Don't you think he might have sat down next to me to talk to me? No man is going to ask for my phone number with my mother right next to me gabbing away about herself!"

My mother said nothing else about John.

We had flown into Los Angeles International Airport, and we took a van back to my parents' house in south Orange County. Lynne lived only about fifteen minutes away, so she drove home from there. I had at least a two-hour drive ahead of me, so I spent the night and planned to leave in the morning.

When I awoke the next day, I went out to the living room, which cannot be seen from the kitchen. My parents were talking to each other. I overheard Gretchen tell my father about Konrad's comments regarding adopted children being defective. All I could hear my father say was, "Oh my."

I went back upstairs to my bedroom and waited several minutes. Eventually, my mother left to do some errands. I came down to the kitchen and sat with him at the table. His health was failing, and indeed, his health had been fragile for many years. He had his elbows on the table and his head in his hands as he struggled to eat something. I had seen him like this many times.

We were quiet, but he looked up briefly and said, "Wendy, you're a good Whitaker."

I didn't respond. I didn't know what to say. I knew he wanted to tell me that I was truly family to him and his side of the family, the Whitakers. Those were the last words he ever spoke to me. I soon took off to drive back home to San Diego. He passed away several months later in June 1998.

I returned to San Diego and fell back into my routines. I didn't hear from Gretchen for quite a while and our phone conversations were sporadic at best.

Right around the time that my father passed away, I received a phone call from John Havens. Upon returning to Bardia, he found my entry in the guest book and copied my information. I wanted to take his tour to Kala Pattar to see Mount Everest. I had already made plans for my trips in 1999, but I wanted to go in 2000.

We kept in touch and exchanged phone calls and letters. He would say, "Come back, love, come back to Nepal. Let me show you the most wonderful places, away from the tourist hotels. Come back, Wendy." I received wonderful postcards from him in Nepal and stored them away as heartfelt mementos. I began making plans to take a lengthy vacation in 2000 to return to Nepal.

5

Sexual Harassment

I began my early career at an investment banking firm working with municipal bonds. However, I soon left the world of Wall Street due to the ubiquitous sexual harassment. Eventually, I landed on Main Street in a sector that employs far more women and experiences far less groping and being locked in an office and chased around the desk.

Sexual harassment is a serious problem, one in which I believe the current laws make worse. If a woman rejects the advance, then the race is on. Can the harasser fire or force out the target before a lawsuit? Or, will the victim get the abuser fired first? The harasser needs to discredit the woman in the worst way possible; he needs to desperately dictate the narrative of a he said/she said event. Often, a serial harasser possesses the capability to persecute his target by stealth or by furtively enlisting others to launch devastating smear campaigns. It is particularly devastating when the enlisted are other women, and some harassers are extremely adept at manipulating those women into attacking a perceived enemy. In my experience, those women are typically gossipers who possess little to no critical thinking skills.

This is what happened to me when I accepted a position as a civilian employee in the U.S. Navy in mid-1998 right around the time my father passed away. I had been working for about six months when I received a promotion and transfer to another base on which a profit center business had been operating for several years at a net loss. In sending me, the District Manager assured me that the top two current managers would be gone before I arrived. He did not hesitate to spread the word about the upcoming changes, so the two soon-to-be ousted managers knew of the upcoming negative employment actions. I would report to a new General Manager.

However, after moving to my new town and arriving on site for my first day at my new position, I discovered that something had gone awry. The old managers remained in their positions, although the DM continued to assure me they would both be gone soon.

It was a hostile environment from the outset. Neither of them wanted me there. The DM had made it clear to both of them to leave me alone. Matters worsened when I discovered within a few days of arriving precisely why the business ran at a net loss. It incurred millions of dollars in inventory shortages every year. The General Manager had moved the receiving activities to an offsite, remote location with no security cameras or security personnel. I knew the newly installed information system well enough to demonstrate that shipments had arrived on the base, but then disappeared without a trace.

In this hostile environment, I shared an office with another manager of the same rank, a woman named Sandy. Someone had converted a stockroom into this space away from the executive offices. We both had been banished to this unworkable spot, presumably to ensure we would both fail.

Sometime in the first few months, a male colleague, Frank, came into our office to chat. I had a photo on my desk from a kayaking expedition in the Sea of Cortez that I had taken the previous summer. He picked up the photo off my desk.

"If I was ever going to cheat on my wife, I would want it to be with Wendy," he said.

It was an awkward moment. Still, I believed at the time that he regretted the poor comment immediately. I was prepared to let it go. However, Sandy ran with it. Soon, she had spread rumors of an alleged affair between Frank and me. Her gossipy girlfriends in the office joined her. Given the planned change over in management, I assumed that once the new General Manager arrived, the tone would change as well. I ignored the silly gossip as best I could.

The change in management did take place finally in the sixth month of my term there. The new GM, Sam, and I interacted very well, and he told me he had been informed he could trust me to run my business well without supervision. In addition, he moved my office into the office adjacent to his, one that had previously belonged to the manager who ranked just above me, but was now gone.

Soon after his arrival, he hired another woman into a position equivalent to mine, but with responsibilities over a different division. Jeannette had been an hourly employee ranked two grades below with an unsatisfactory performance review. For some unknown reason, she received a promotion to senior manager level. However, she was soon in over her head and failed an Inspector General audit of the business. This was an audit the new GM had requested to establish a baseline from which his performance could be judged. Everyone else, including me, was surprised by the IG visit. My division passed with flying colors.

Terry was Sam's administrative assistant and one of the women who enthusiastically spread the vicious gossip about the alleged affair. She and Jeannette teamed up with Sandy and several other women to do so. In those first few months, the sexual harassment was perpetrated by my own sex. They committed the same type of egregious harassment against another woman who worked there. She was a good worker who spoke little English. They spread rumors that she was a prostitute. These women were vicious. I was soon walking a tightrope between them all, but still my working relationship with Sam remained solid.

However, several months later, he suggested dinner together to talk business. Unfortunately, he had no real business to discuss. He made advances and suggested playing along would result in a promotion. I refused. He retaliated. He launched and waged a smear campaign in response. That silly gossip about an alleged affair became his weapon, and the gossipy women became his combatants.

He twisted what happened and called me the sexual predator. He spread lies all the way up to the C-Suite that I was having illicit affairs, and the sexually hostile environment proved so pervasive that sexually graphic graffiti about me and Frank showed up in the women's bathrooms repeatedly—women's not men's bathrooms.

If other people were around, Sam was unfailingly polite and respectful to me. However, when the executive office was empty except for the two of us, he subjected me to a barrage of profanity and demands that I leave, He threw things at me. He threw pencils, pens, staplers, books, and folders. Once he grabbed a 4" three-ring binder full of operating statements. He threw that at me, and it hit me in the chest.

I didn't know what else to do but find another job. I intended to move back home to San Diego, and the long-distance job search took longer than expected. I approached the HR manager, a woman in her 60s and close to retirement, and I explained the harassment, especially the incidents of graffiti, thrown books, and office items. I begged for a transfer.

"If there are no witnesses, it's your word against his, and he's the GM" was her only response.

I had already postponed my trip to Nepal from 1999 to 2000 since I had other vacation plans. However, life intervened again. Sam was getting pushback from above and he cancelled all vacations for the end of 2000. I called John Havens and cancelled my trip to Nepal.

"No, love, come on this trip!" he said.

"I can't. You wouldn't believe how abusive this boss is. If he has cancelled vacations, I can't get around it. Put me down for spring definitely."

"Wendy, come on this trip! Wendy, love, you must come this time!" he was adamant. But, I couldn't do it without risking my job.

I called him in February of 2001. I told him I was sending a deposit for the trip.

There was a long, long silent pause.

"Wendy, last fall was my last trip to Nepal. I didn't know how to tell you this. I have a tumor in my brain, and it's malignant. I call it the alien in my brain. That was my farewell trip. I have been on chemo, and you wouldn't recognize me. I have gained so much weight, and the tumor has crushed my left eye. I wear an eye patch now. The doctors say no more than six months."

I was so shocked. I don't recall what I said or the rest of the conversation, except that he told me he was considering going to India. He knew of a doctor there who treated brain tumors by administering the chemo through the nostrils directly into the brain.

There were one or two more phone calls and some emails as we stayed in touch with one another with increasing infrequency.

6

Puppets and Puppeteers

During this time, Konrad passed away in March 2001 at the age of 93. When I heard the news, a thought immediately flashed through my head: "He got away with it."

Rather than ask Sam for time off to attend the funeral, I asked the HR Manager. She informed him that I would be attending a family funeral.

The family held the funeral at his last full-time church, the same church I attended as a child, Christ Lutheran Church in Covina. I drove to my mother's house to pick her up and drive her to the service. During the ride, she repeatedly expressed adoring acclaim for her father.

The church had built a new sanctuary, and Konrad's portrait hung in the narthex as the founding pastor. While waiting outside the sanctuary for the memorial to commence, we were greeted by the current senior pastor, Dennis. He had been hired there as an associate pastor when I was a young teenager. He was still at the same church after so many years.

He expressed his condolences, and then he asked me what church I attended. I told him I had moved over to the Presbyterian church many years ago.

"Traitor!" he retorted.

I thought he meant it as a joke, but I wasn't sure. It was odd though. His background was Swedish, and when first hired, he fielded many jokes about being in the wrong Lutheran church—German rather than Swedish.

I excused myself to meander around the premise. The old sanctuary had been converted to a library or some other function. The Alice Koosmann Memorial Garden was gone. Returning to that site brought back many memories, and I walked around the church campus reminiscing about my childhood, Sunday school, confirmation, and sitting quietly through many of Konrad's sermons. One specific sermon came back to me, not so much because of its insights, rather because he repeated it so often.

Konrad used the Book of Ruth in the Bible as the basis for many of his wedding ceremony sermons. In the story, Naomi was a widow and had two sons. Both sons were married. The two sons died, and the daughters-in-law had differing responses to the blow dealt them. Naomi urged each young woman to go home to her mother and remarry. Orpah kissed Naomi goodbye and left for home. Ruth did not.

"But Ruth clung tightly to Naomi. 'Look,' Naomi said to her, "your sister-in-law has gone back to her people and to her gods. You should do the same.'

"But Ruth replied, 'Don't ask me to leave you and turn back. Wherever you go, I will go; wherever you live, I will live. Your people will be my people, and your God will be my God. Wherever you die, I will die, and there I will be buried. May the Lord punish me severely if I allow anything but death to separate us!' When Naomi saw that Ruth was determined to go with her, she said nothing more." Ruth 1: 14-18

Konrad interpreted this scripture as a directive for all women to follow their husbands and obey them. He didn't see it as a story of a woman and her daughter-in-law. I always thought it was a twisted interpretation that used other women to guilt a new bride into submission. Besides, I have always wondered why Ruth preferred her mother-in-law to her own mother.

I went back to the sanctuary and sat next to Gretchen in the pew. The memorial suited a former Bishop, although it seemed surreal to me. The coffin had lovely flowers draped over it. We sang hymns. The current Bishop gave a homily. Several pastors gave eulogies, and the eulogies were all very high praise of Konrad. Pastor Dennis, who possessed an excellent singing voice, sang a solo of the hymn, "The Old Rugged Cross."

The tributes included some specific numbers that intrigued me. One pastor quoted how many members were added to the American Lutheran Church Pacific Region under Konrad as Bishop. I don't recall the number, but it was to the very person...rather than a rounded off number or an approximate percentage gain in membership.

It was noted that Konrad sometimes acted as the chaplain for the Los Angeles Dodgers. That tribute included some detailed information on Konrad's cousin, Jerry Koosman, who had pitched for the New York Mets. This part of the eulogy sounded as if Konrad himself was personally responsible for the Miracle Mets of '69 and their stunning win in the World Series that year. Jerry pitched two of the winning games in the series. It also contained very precise information about the amount of money he had contributed to his sisters' college tuition. The amount was down to the penny even though it had been 60 or 70 years ago.

I sat next to my mother, and I was numb. I wondered what she thought. I wondered if I would ever reach a point of talking to her about the abuse, not in anger but hopefully to find comfort and commiseration, to find sympathy rather than rejection. I already knew the answer from our trip to Nepal. Gretchen would take up her father's defense unwaveringly. I already knew that the door had been shut after the way I approached the issue in anger.

Sitting in the pew at Konrad's funeral, for first time ever, it occurred to me that perhaps she had been a victim as well. If so, her unwavering defense of her father baffled me. A young child who has been sexually violated doesn't wonder if it happened to mommy too. It's a lonesome experience, and the child typically assumes she is the bad person. Many times, the abuser will threaten the child with punishment for telling or demand that they keep it a secret. The child is filled with pain and terror. Wondering if it has happened to others simply doesn't occur. Children that young find it difficult to verbalize a horror they cannot understand. However, as an adult, I learned that there is rarely only one victim in a family.

Gretchen socialized and played the role of grieving daughter very well. She repeated many times that Konrad had a long life, and it was time to go home to Christ as friends expressed their condolences. She hadn't seen many of the people in years, so there was a lot of catching up to do with long-time friends who had known her and the Koosmann family.

After the reception, I drove her back to her house. During the ride home, she expressed praise for the funeral service. I asked her how anybody could possibly know the precise dollar amount of tuition that Konrad had paid for his sisters.

"It was exactly as he wanted it, exactly as he planned it. They all did so well. He even wrote the whole service," she said.

"He planned it? What does that mean? You mean he had several people he wanted to be asked if they would participate?" I asked incredulously.

"Oh, much more than that. He wrote all the eulogies himself, and he designated who would read which eulogies. They all agreed to do it as he requested," she said.

Konrad wrote his own eulogies and determined in advance who would deliver which statements. Suddenly they were all nothing but puppets to me. It reminded me of the gospel of John, in which Jesus speaks of Satan as a liar and the father of lies. Satan doesn't fight against the church; he joins the church. Every man who played a role in the theatrical presentation of Konrad's life and accomplishments that day enabled the evil one to speak his lies under the cloak of righteousness. Still, this was 2001, before The Boston Globe published the first stories of sexual abuse by priests in Boston. No one would have believed that Konrad was a child molester.

And Konrad, in true abuser fashion, dictated the final narrative about himself even from the grave.

After I returned to work, my boss adopted a new tactic. He couldn't ding me on performance, so he switched to conduct. My nerves were overwrought from the harassment and constant vigilance on the job. I couldn't afford a single mistake. I made perfection a requirement, and for months on end, I worked from 5:00 a.m. to at least 7:00 p.m., seven days a week. I had no personal life at all, and the stress took a deep toll on my physical health.

In addition, the Inspector General made another surprise audit to determine if the deficiencies he had found previously had been remedied. This audit had not been requested by the GM. He was also surprised. My division had no deficiencies to correct, and still passed easily. However, Jeannette had not made any corrections from the previous audit, and the IG found more problems. He called her out badly by name in the report, and the report was public.

This embarrassment gave both Jeannette and Terry more reason to tear me down. Rather than focus on fixing her deficiencies, Jeannette, along with Terry, set out to make me look bad in order to deflect any more attention to the failed IG audit. They spent their days scheming and assisting Sam with his harassment. I spent my days maintaining perfection at work and looking for another job at the same time.

I was at work on September 11, 2001. I remember well the footage of the two planes flying into the World Trade Center and their resulting implosion. The base went into Threatcon Delta, and the Commanding Officer sent home all non-essential personnel during the emergency. I was considered essential personnel, so I stayed. My boss was back east for a conference. He returned once flights resumed after having been grounded due to the attack.

On September 12, John Havens called me while I was at work on the Navy base. I could hear the weakness and pain in his voice. He asked how I was, if I knew of anyone affected by the attacks. He expressed his deep sorrow and sympathy on behalf of himself and England. I was gripped with grief that he would think of me and call to make sure I was safe even as he was dying.

The harassment stopped for a couple of weeks after Sam returned. But, one day he called me into his office, and the HR manager was there. He formally accused me of misconduct, of being AWOL on the day of 9/11. The personnel action said I would be fired immediately if I could not be found or if I failed to respond to my beeper or a page over the PA. I had been present that day at work on September 11, and I could prove it. I refused to sign the adverse employment action, and he threatened to take further personnel action for refusing to acknowledge the document with my signature.

I discovered later than Jeannette and Terry had led the attack against me by signing witness statements that I couldn't be found on 9/11. They claimed to have repeatedly called my pager, and I didn't respond. When I checked the records, there were no incoming calls. In his haste to force me out, Sam failed to double check the women's accusations.

I left his office looking calm and collected, but in a severe panic attack. My mouth literally went dry. I began shaking badly. However, I made it over to a phone in another part of the building and placed a call to the EEO Officer to initiate a sexual harassment complaint.

Sam backed off once I started that process. However, Jeannette and Terry increased their efforts to destroy me. It was during this time that I learned that Sam had been attacking Frank's performance as well, but Frank reported up a different chain of command. Frank's boss was pleased with his performance.

The day after I received the letter of misconduct, Frank called me to his office. Once I was there, he shut the door.

He sat down at his desk, while I stood. He had a surreal look on his face.

"I'm just telling you this as a courtesy. I received a voice message on my answering machine here. It was a man's voice, but I didn't recognize it. He said, 'We know where you're going, and we know what you're doing, and we're going to take out Wendy and you're going down with her,'" he said.

"What does that mean?" I asked.

"I'm just telling you as a courtesy," he replied.

"Let me hear the message. It could mean a variety of things," I responded.

"I'm just telling you as a courtesy," he repeated.

"No, seriously, let me hear the whole message. Let me hear the context of what was said. Maybe I recognize the voice."

"I'm just telling you as a courtesy."

Whatever I said to him, his only response was to say, "I'm just telling you as a courtesy."

At that moment, I almost threw up right in his office. My nerves were nearly destroyed. His facial expression struck me as pure evil. I got out of there quickly, went to my desk, typed a brief resignation letter, and then went to my boss and handed that letter to him. He accepted it gleefully. I walked out for good, and I told no one where I was going.

7

Life on La Cresta Drive

I packed up and went home to San Diego. A friend let me flop at his home while I searched for a permanent place to live. Within a few weeks, I rented an apartment suite in a private home in Point Loma. The owner, Julie, traveled extensively for business, and she always had a tenant to ensure the house was well cared for in her frequent absence.

A friend had referred me to her, so she accepted me over the phone as a tenant without question. I drove to her house on La Cresta Drive and parked my car. This area of the neighborhood had very steep hills. Her garage was at ground level, but her house, a small white cottage, was halfway up the hill. A lovely winding path made of weathered bricks led me to the front door.

A beautiful woman in her mid-50s opened the door and introduced herself as Julie. From the very first impression, she was the epitome of friendly exuberance. She invited me in, and I was surprised by the home. The original home had been small, just a two bedroom/one bathroom cottage. But she had pushed the back wall out for more room and built a staircase up the hill with a den and bedrooms off to the right. A massive master bedroom was at the top. The back wall, the wall up the staircase and the master bedroom wall facing the backyard were all floor-to-ceiling glass French doors. She had no window coverings on them at all. No blinds or curtains. This was the closest thing I had ever seen to a glass house.

She showed me the original two bedrooms and bathroom just off the front door, which were my areas with French doors out to the side patio. She explained that she was leaving in just a few minutes for a week, and she gave me a key.

"Make yourself at home. This is now your home as well. When you bring your things over, drive up Bill and Ginny's driveway and park. Then you can just walk across on level ground rather than climbing the stairs."

She showed me the neighbor's house, which was at the same level on the hill as hers. They had built their driveway up the hill with a carport under the home. A short path connected the two properties.

"It's ok. I do it all the time, especially with groceries. We've been doing it for thirty years. Oh, by the way, Bob lives here too. He's my companion, but he travels as much as I do. Usually, he just goes up to the master bedroom from the backyard rather than use the front door. I'll be back Saturday night, but I leave again Sunday morning for another week."

She grabbed her suitcase, caught the taxi waiting for her on the street, and took off. I went back to my friend's place and packed my car. When I got back to La Cresta Drive, I hesitated about driving up the driveway when the people inside didn't know me. I looked at the steep staircase I would have to climb. Then, I drove up the driveway and parked the car. No one came out of the house. I didn't get any disapproving looks through the windows. In fact, it seemed that no one was home.

Once done, I parked on the street and went in to get to know my new home. Julie had beautiful furnishings that spanned French Provincial and Italian Provence styles. The kitchen was clad in cobalt blue, white, and brilliant yellows while the living room, right off my rooms, was in lavenders, pale yellows, and mint greens. I wandered around getting comfortable. Then I went to the grocery store for some staples.

The next morning, I went out to the kitchen to make coffee. I was wearing nothing but a silk chemise and standing at the sink when I saw a little old man amble by the window that faced the side walkway. He looked a bit like George Burns in cargo pants but without the cigar and glasses. He turned the corner and opened one of the French doors and came right in. He set a paper bag on the counter before he noticed me.

"Oh, you must be Julie's new tenant. I'm Bill from next door. I brought over oranges from my tree, and I'm going to get some lemons from Julie's tree. We always do this. Help yourself to oranges. And come by today around 4 for cocktail time. The door is always unlocked, and we always just come and go as we want to. Just walk on in. Everybody else does. OK, so I'll see you this afternoon."

He ambled out the French door, which I then knew was always unlocked. I watched through the glass doors as he went up the back path and picked a few lemons off the tree. Then he came down and went back to his house.

He never asked my name or seemed to notice my chemise. This was my introduction to Life on La Cresta Drive. Around 4 p.m., I walked across the path and took the steps to their front door. I knocked. Two voices from within yelled, "Come in!"

The door was unlocked. I walked into a small landing with a few stairs leading up to the main house. At the top was the kitchen counter. The living room was to the right, and the breakfast area and hallway to the bedrooms to the left.

Bill was sitting at the kitchen counter facing the door. He scolded me.

"Hey, I told you to just come on in. You don't need to knock. Now, would you like a glass of wine? I have red or white."

I stood there like an idiot. There were two other people sitting at the kitchen counter as well. Bill spoke to me like we were old friends. He didn't introduce me to the others; indeed, he didn't know my name.

The woman spoke up.

"I'm Ginny. Come on and sit down. Once you have a glass of wine at our counter, you're family! Julie told us you were moving in."

She was very welcoming and friendly. And, she wore a black top and pants, but the most colorful bohemian cape over it. Her makeup and manicure were perfect.

"I'm Wendy. I just moved in yesterday."

The other person at the counter was a man who was looking at me very intently. He was very athletic and very handsome with perfect blonde hair and vivid blue eyes. He stuck out his hand to shake.

"I'm Werner."

He started to say something else, but Bill interrupted him.

"Listen, you are making a big mistake. If you make the trip over to Nepal, then you should do Everest, not Ama Dablam. This might be your last chance. Why waste it on Ama Dablam?"

"You're going to Nepal? I was there in 1997. It's stunningly beautiful," I said.

"Yes, I've been there before," Werner said nonchalantly. Then he replied to Bill.

"Everest is a walk up. There's no technical climbing. No rock climbing. No ice climbing. It's a walk up."

I had never heard anyone describe Mount Everest as a walk up. I wanted to ask about his plans, but Ginny started talking to me.

"Let me show you the house." She got down from her bar stool, grabbed her cane, and walked over to a wall between the sliding door out to the patio and the hallway to the bedrooms. There were dozens of antique hand farm implements hanging on that wall.

"Now these belonged to Bill's grandfather from before the Civil War. Bill's from Georgia. He still thinks he's some old Georgia farm boy. Let me show you my artwork."

She took me out the sliding door and up the hill to her studio. She showed me her massive collection of brightly colored, abstract art. All of them were beautiful.

"I know what Picasso was trying to do with the Cubist movement. I liked him."

I was uncertain about what I just heard. She seemed old enough to have known Picasso himself.

"Did you know Picasso?"

"No, but I knew Winston Churchill," she replied. "Let's go back to the kitchen. Werner's not married, you know. He was married to our daughter, but they got divorced. Where are you from? Is your family in Point Loma? I guess you're not married either since you are renting from Julie. That's good. Who needs a man anyway? Women can do just fine on their own."

In that one afternoon while having a cocktail with Bill and Ginny and Werner, I learned what the neighborhood already knew. Bill and Ginny were the glue that held everyone together on La Cresta Drive. In a couple of short hours, I knew their stories.

They were in their 80s, and both had been involved in WWII. Bill was a Navy fighter pilot in the Pacific theater during the war, and he was shot down over the Pacific Ocean by the enemy Japanese.

I never did hear the story of his rescue out of the water, but I heard him say many times over the years,

"I had to eject from my cockpit."

Ginny quickly married her high school sweetheart before he went north to Canada. The U.S. had not yet entered the war, and he wanted to fight the Nazis. He joined the Canadian Royal Air Force, which sent him to the European theater as a fighter pilot. Only a few weeks later, Ginny received notice that he had been shot down over Germany. She had no other news.

In her grief, she went to work for the U.S. State Department, which stationed her in London during the Blitz. She told many stories of meeting Winston Churchill as he walked through the hallways of the State Department with a bottle of scotch under his arm. When the Berlin Wall finally fell in November of 1989, Bill took Ginny to East Germany to search for news of her first husband. They found his grave in a Lutheran church cemetery, properly marked and cared for.

They took me in without question as I tried to recover from chaos and harassment. As I left that day, Werner asked if I like to go rock climbing. He invited me to go with him and his friends that weekend to go climbing in Baja. I told him maybe another time and no, I didn't know how to rock climb. I enjoyed mountain climbing though. But I was just back in San Diego and was thinking of heading to Anza Borrego that weekend.

As I returned to Julie's home from my initiation into Life on La Cresta Drive, I knew I had to get busy. I needed to find a job, and I needed to let go of what I had just left. La Cresta Drive was peaceful, and I felt safer. But I was frightened by what had happened at the Navy. There were people in that area of the base who belonged to gangs and were committing some serious internal theft. I didn't know who all of them were, but I'm sure they knew I could pinpoint anomalies through the information system.

I took out a P.O. Box in Escondido, a town in north San Diego about 20 miles away. No one other than one or two friends had my street address, not even family. The friends who knew where I was had no affiliation with the military. I changed my cell phone carrier and took out a new number. I did not install a landline. Julie, as the owner of the house paid the utilities, so the deed and utilities were in her name.

Even though I left, I continued on with the sexual harassment complaint against my boss. A few weeks after my initiation into Life on La Cresta Drive, I received a phone call on my new cell phone number. It was Frank from the Navy base.

"How did you get my number?" I demanded to know.

"Wendy, you sound so stressed. You don't sound like yourself. Just relax. Just let go of everything, and you'll be so much happier. Just let go. Let go of it," he said.

"What are you talking about? How did you get my number?"

"Seriously, I can hear your nerves through the phone. Just drop everything. You need your peace of mind. Let go of it."

"I don't know what you're talking about."

"The complaint. It's making you so unhappy. Just drop the harassment complaint. Drop it, let go of it."

"I'm not dropping the complaint." I exclaimed.

To this day, I have had to rely upon some conjecture. My sexual harassment complaint was against Sam, not Frank. Perhaps Frank believed I named him in the complaint because of his unfortunate quip about wanting to have an affair with me. Or, perhaps others had complained about the graffiti and named him. I didn't know. But I did know that he sounded weird, and I remembered what he said about a phone message taking me out. Now, he pressured me to withdraw my discrimination complaint, which meant he was retaliating.

He raised his voice and began to sound angry.

"Wendy, drop the complaint. Drop it. If you don't drop it, I will have to come to San Diego and shoot you."

He knew I had gone back to San Diego.

"I'm not dropping it. Leave me alone. I don't want to hear from you ever again."

He went berserk on the phone. He screamed at me like a crazy man.

"I'm watching you. I'm having your car followed. I have covert cameras surrounding your house. Covert cameras in space. Cameras on satellites. I know what you're doing. I have covert cameras on satellites watching your house and your every move. I'll always know wherever you go and whatever you do…"

I hung up the phone in the middle of his sentence.

Two days later, I received a letter in the mail at my street address, not my P.O. Box. It was postmarked at that Navy base on the same day as the call. Inside was a letter sized paper, which was tri-folded to fit the envelope. Scrawled in block letters on the outside, a message read:

"I HOPE ALL IS WELL"

I opened it and found five satellite photos of Julie's house cut out and pasted onto the paper.

He knew where I lived.

I was now beyond anxiety. I was deeply frightened. I showed the letter to a friend. He said, "It's a threat, call the police." I called the police. They said, "It's through the mail. It's not our jurisdiction. Take it to the Postal Inspector." I took it to the Postal Inspector, a nice gentleman in his 50s. When he saw it, he became very alarmed.

"Oh my God, oh my God. If you feel like your life is in danger, call the FBI. This is a threat, a threat through the mail. Call the FBI if you feel like your life is in danger! Call the FBI!"

My life felt way too surreal to call the FBI, but I did, although I felt weird doing so. The FBI was for organized crime or gangs in my mind. I grew up in a family that had no need to call the police. That would bring stigma on our middle class, devout Christian family. After placing the call, I tried to calm my nerves and packed for my excursion to Anza Borrego.

8

My Ally of Oriflamme Canyone

Not more than a two-hour drive from San Diego, Anza Borrego is an outdoor playground for those who like to hike, camp, and explore. During rainy years, the desert floor becomes a blanket of vivid colors as desert wildflowers bloom en masse for only a few weeks. The Palm Canyon trail is a popular, easy hike that leads hikers to a beautiful desert spring surrounded by palm trees. And, the Santa Rosa/San Jacinto mountain range borders the desert floor to the east with many famous peaks to climb: Rabbit, San Gorgonio, Mount San Jacinto, 8562, and Villager among others. On the other side of the range lie Palm Springs, the Salton Sea, and Joshua Tree National Park.

I needed some time to myself, and I wanted seclusion. I had no plans for a campsite, although I had reservations at the developed site adjacent to Palm Canyon and Indian Head Peak just in case. I took off around 5:00 a.m. with my gear and an old, worn out map.

I headed south down Highway S2 and eventually pulled over to the side. I wasn't sure about which way to go, but I knew I wanted to stay away from Whale Peak, certain to be a favorite with hikers and visitors looking for the ancient Indian pictographs. I got back on the road and drove slowly looking west for any kind of trail.

I passed what seemed to be an old abandoned road in a wash, but it was faint. A faded sign said "Oriflamme Wash." The map showed no markings for it. Perfect! I turned down the wash.

I drove slowly trying to stay on the wash, which frequently disappeared. The driving was difficult; deep sand, huge boulders, and debris from the years of flash floods blocked my way, and I had to navigate around the obstacles. I had an old Ford Ranger pickup, which did just fine in the difficult terrain as long as I drove under 10 mph.

The trail began gaining altitude, and soon I was looking into a small depression to the left. There appeared to be cottonwoods, but how odd in this particular part of Anza Borrego. Suddenly, the trail took a sharp left turn and headed down a hill. At the bottom was the most exquisite oasis, a running creek with a small waterfall, grassy banks and several dozen cottonwoods providing shade around the pond. I parked the truck and pitched my tent in the sand.

The day was perfect, not too hot, and I enjoyed the exploring. When dusk fell, I made a light supper, had a glass of wine, and sat peacefully enjoying the sound of the waterfall and the solitude of my little oasis. Later, I fell asleep easily in my tent.

Very late in the night, violent winds awakened me. The gusts were at least 30 to 40 miles per hour. Luckily, I had secured my tent well. Even so, I wondered if I were not inside to help hold the tent down, would it have flown away?

The banshee wind howled mystically through the small chasm. The cottonwoods acted as vocal cords for the gushes of air blasting in from the west, and a full moon lit up my summer-weight tent through the netting.

The howling continued, but suddenly I was aware of footsteps circling my tent. I could hear them despite the wind. Every hair on my body stood on end, and I froze with terror. They were most definitely human footsteps I heard pacing around my tent. I had my rifle with me, but even so I could not find my voice or the courage to get out of the tent to confront the intruder.

Eventually the footsteps stopped. I fell asleep around daybreak and had the most fantastical dreams.

When I awoke, the sun was overhead and the winds had completely died. The silence rattled me. I gingerly unzipped the tent door and stepped outside.

Rings and rings of coyote tracks circled my tent.

A coyote! I had to laugh at myself. Coyotes are fairly harmless to adult humans. In ancient Indian legends, the coyote spirit animal symbolized the trickster, a transformer, or a shapeshifter. They are bold, fearless, crafty, rebellious, and spunky. When a spirit coyote enters our awareness, it brings high-voltage, higher levels of conscious clarity. Their cleverness is renown, and their instincts are well honed.

At that moment I felt a kinship with the coyote who visited me that night, although I didn't know why. He was my protector in the desert. My ally in Oriflamme Canyon.

I found out later that in this particular area of Anza Borrego, illegal gold mining continues especially with cyanide. Those who venture into the area have occasionally been shot at for daring to explore. My coyote kept me safe that night. And while I didn't know it at the time, he predicted that I was in store for those high voltage, higher levels of conscious clarity later that year.

I drove back to San Diego a little early in the afternoon and headed over to Bill and Ginny's kitchen counter. I wanted to tell them about my coyote. I didn't bother knocking; I just walked right in. They were both at the kitchen counter.

"Do you want red or white?" Bill asked.

We chatted about my camping trip and how my job hunt was progressing. After about 15 minutes, Werner popped in and joined the conversation. Then another neighbor dropped by and another. Pretty soon, the talk turned to politics and the attack on 9/11.

"Listen, Bush is going to ruin this country," Bill exclaimed. "Al Gore would have known what to do. We don't need a war. Bush stole the election."

"Well, I guess I should fess up that I lean conservative," I said.

"That's ok, but we're Democrats through and through. And Bush is going to ruin this country."

I wasn't sure about delving into politics, but I soon discovered that Bill and Ginny were similar to my family in that differing opinions were respected. Then you voted.

"I want Hillary to be President," said Ginny.

"Hillary? Clinton?" I was astonished. "I'm sorry, but I can't respect her. She should have divorced Bill after the Lewinsky mess. Look how he humiliated her in front of the entire world. No, I think Hillary stayed with Bill just for a power grab. But you may get your wish. In my opinion, that's why she ran for Senator in New York, as a launch platform for a presidential bid."

"No, she stayed with Bill to hold her family together. That's more important," Ginny insisted. "She held her family together."

The men were now talking about climbing and hiking. Ginny and I continued talking about Hillary.

"What about Paula Jones and Juanita Broaddrick? What if Bill really raped Juanita? Then Hillary is sticking with a rapist for a husband," I asked her.

"Juanita denied it at first, then she changed her story," Ginny said. "She just wanted publicity."

"I would find it hard to believe a woman would do that for publicity. Who would speak out against a man in power? Clinton was the Governor of Arkansas. He could have crushed her," I replied.

I wanted to press her on this one. Ginny was an ardent feminist. But her version was the original version of feminism that pushed for women's suffrage, equal pay for equal work, dropping the word "obey" from women's marriage vows, and repealing the coverture laws. She didn't ascribe to the "burn all men" versions from women like Valerie Solanas.

However, Werner interrupted. Bill was getting up from the kitchen counter.

"Let me show you something," Werner said to me.

I went outside with the men to the side of Bill's house. Leaning against the wall was a huge kayak with three seats. It had to be 25 feet long.

"Do you like kayaking? I'm planning to kayak out to Sunset Cliffs to go lobster diving. I have my own single kayak, but if you want to come along, this kayak fits at least two people," he said.

I had given up practicing strict vegetarianism, so lobster sounded good. I agreed to go. He told me to be ready the following Saturday morning. He would get the kayak from Bill around 8:00 a.m.

I met Werner at Bill's on Saturday morning and helped him lift that huge kayak on top of his red Jeep Cherokee. Then I got in, and we drove down to Shelter Island to the boat launch. We got the kayak into the water, climbed in, and paddled out to the end of the point. We rounded the corner of the point into the ocean side of the peninsula and found a small sandy beach along Sunset Cliffs to land and start diving for lobster.

Since it was January, the water was very chilly, and neither of us had a wetsuit. I managed to dive for a while but got out frequently to warm up before diving back into the waves. The cold didn't seem to bother Werner at all. We were very successful and caught our limit within a couple of hours. He had brought a small cooler and put the lobster in for transport back. We changed back into dry clothes using the popular surfer method of changing with a towel on. Then, we sat on the beach for a while talking.

He was divorced, as Ginny had told me, with two daughters, and he was a geologist. He loved rock climbing, mountain climbing, kayaking, biking, running, swimming the cove, triathlons, sailing, diving, the list went on and on. He even had a pilot's license and had owned his own plane at one time.

I told him a little about what had happened at the Navy and why I came back to San Diego. I wanted to be as truthful as I could.

"I started here in San Diego, but I got transferred to another base. It was a really stressful job, and my boss hit up on me. I've never experienced such extreme harassment, not even in the brokerage industry. I still have nightmares about it."

We hit it off very quickly, and he was very easy to talk to. By then it was clear that he was interested in me. I kept the possibility open, especially since John was dying from cancer before we ever got a chance to explore our attraction to each other.

I went into the details about my boss throwing things at me and the satellite photo letter. I told him that I was scared.

"They're bullies. I don't like bullies. I learned early as a child to be the bigger bully to scare them into leaving me alone," he said.

"Well, that's not me," I replied.

"Maybe not, but you didn't have my background. I was born in Germany in 1946 right after the war. My mother, Helga, was married and her husband went off to fight. After the war ended, she waited for him to come home, but never heard from him. She couldn't find any information at all. There were so many dead soldiers, so she assumed he had died in the war.

"She took up with another man and got pregnant with me. They weren't married, but one day her husband showed up suddenly from being MIA. He wasn't dead, and he wasn't happy to find his wife pregnant by another man. He kicked her out and divorced her. My biological father didn't stick around, so she was a single mom at a bad time. It was a real stigma.

"Eventually, she married an American soldier and we emigrated here. I was ten years old, and we landed first in the Bronx before moving south to Louisiana and Alabama. The neighborhood was mostly Jewish, so it was a fight a day. That's why I learned how to beat bullies."

"What about you? What's your story?" he wanted to know.

"I'm adopted. My adopted mother's family is originally from Germany. My dad's side goes back to the Mayflower."

"Did you ever try to find your real mom?"

"No, I looked into it. Adoptions in California at the time were sealed. It's nearly impossible and would take thousands of dollars in attorney fees."

"You should still try," he said.

We packed up and launched the kayak into the waves. The kayak was so big, it held the cooler inside the storage section with ease. We paddled back to Shelter Island, returned the kayak to Bill, and divvied the lobster after leaving some for Bill and Ginny. As I left to go back to Julie's house, he asked me out for dinner the following Friday night. I said yes, and that's how we started dating. He was 17 years my senior, but we both had our own story of origins. And, we both loved being outside and active.

Later that week, I received a phone call from a woman who identified herself as an FBI agent. She said she had looked into the letter and spoken to Frank.

"He said it was just a joke. He was just trying to spook you. He was just joking. So, you don't have to worry."

I was stunned. Two men saw the letter and each expressed considerable alarm. They insisted I report it to the right law enforcement agency. But that woman took Frank's preposterous explanation hook, line, and sinker. She didn't talk to me about what I thought happened. She simply accepted the harasser's own narrative without question.

My anxiety and fear levels increased exponentially after that satellite photo letter. My nerves were shot, and I began having nightmares night after night. Frequently, I woke myself up screaming from those nightmares. During the day, all I could think about was the sexual harassment. I questioned myself constantly wondering if I could have done anything differently.

9

Mammoth Men I've Known - January 2022

One Saturday morning later that January around 6:00 a.m., I awoke to a loud banging on my front door. I opened the door to see a soft fog washing over the neighborhood in the morning light. My sleepy eyes could barely make out the misty silhouette of my neighbor, Bill. Despite his age, Bill remained physically active with walking, hiking, and lifting weights. He was dressed in camp pants and a hiking vest, and he seemed completely unaware of the hour and my bathrobe.

"Hey, Wendy," Bill said. "The annual ski trip to Mammoth is next week. I know you love to ski. Why don't you come along?"

Bill and his two WWII buddies had been skiing at Mammoth Mountain in the Eastern Sierras annually for over forty years. He became very excited.

"You know, at Mammoth anyone over eighty years old is entitled to free lift tickets. We share a condo, and there is an extra bedroom if you want to come along."

This made an alluring offer for an inexpensive ski trip. But what an odd group we would make, three WWII vets in their mid 80s, and one woman in her late 30s.

I considered the emotional upheaval I was experiencing at the time. I continued having difficulty letting go of the past. My mind replayed scene after scene from the years at the Navy, entire conversations verbatim, as I tried to grasp the scope of what had happened to me. Frequently, I referred to my brain as a "broken record."

I considered all this quickly with Bill standing there at the door waiting for my answer. An escape to the Sierras presented an irresistible diversion. I felt some momentary concern about how this would appear especially to Ginny. Yet my desire to ski and to get up to the mountains outweighed my concern. My previous trips to the Sierras always proved to be refreshing. I expected the same from this trip. I took the offer despite appearances.

"O.K.," Bill said, "we leave tomorrow. By the way, we always cook a large turkey when we arrive. Then we eat that for lunch and dinner all week.

Sunday morning, John arrived to pick up Bill and me. John was gregarious, and very friendly. I think he sensed my reticence to join a group of WWII vets, and he made a valiant effort to put me at ease. We loaded the van with our food and gear. Bill took the driver's seat, and I rode shotgun as we went to pick up Jim. My discomfort with the arrangement began to swell. Even though John seemed happy to have me along, I did not know him or Jim. I could not shake the feeling neither one wanted a woman to go along, but Bill had insisted.

We drove to pick up Jim, who, Bill had informed me, was an engineer. I knew what to expect as my father had been an engineer. They are a different breed, a good breed, as they invent the most useful tools of everyday life as well as sending astronauts to the moon. And they always want to fix whatever is broken. But generally speaking, they are not the most outwardly exuberant people. Jim was true to form, and very quiet.

We took off heading up Highway 15 to 395 north, which skirts the eastern Sierras and heads into Oregon. Bill handed me an envelope with several $20 bills inside.

"Here, you're in charge of the kitty. We all put in $40 each, and all expenses are paid out of the kitty. Then we divide whatever is left over equally. So that way, it's fair to everyone."

This presented me with a problem. The trip had come up so quickly, I had only enough time to go grocery shopping and to pack my clothes. I had not withdrawn any cash from the bank, and I had assumed I could card as I go and get cash in Mammoth.

I said nothing to the men about this. I felt a bit embarrassed to be caught unprepared, and I considered my dilemma quietly.

When we reached Four Corners at the junction of 395 and Highway 58, we pulled into the gas station to refuel the van. Bill told me to go pay for the gas with money from the kitty.

Quickly, I made some mental computations. It takes two tanks of gas to get there, two tanks to get back, for a total of four tanks. There were four of us, thus I was responsible for one tank. Since I had not contributed to the kitty, I surreptitiously slid my credit card out of my wallet, and I went into the station to pay for the gas.

I surreptitiously slid back into the van. Bill started the engine and we continued heading north up 395.

Without warning, Bill asked me how much money was left in the kitty. I panicked. I stuttered. The cat was out of the bag, so to speak. When Bill discovered the truth, he yelled at me.

"Hey, you broke the rules! Listen, we've been doing this for forty years and we always do it this way so it's fair to everyone."

Jim joined in and was scolding me too. John appeared to be enjoying the scene, although he took my side, and he tried to convince Bill and Jim to go easy on me. I tried to explain the logic behind my decision. Trying to reason with the men did not help. I had broken the rules. I wondered how many more unspoken rules existed.

"Well, that's what you get for inviting a girl along!" I said. "How am I supposed to know the rules, if you don't tell me upfront?"

Apparently, Bill had no response, because he glared at me in silent exasperation.

The rest of the road trip went smoothly, although I remained very quiet. I tend to be on the quiet side, although I am comfortable stepping out of my quietness to initiate and join in on conversations. However, I clammed up after the rule breaking incident.

We arrived in Mammoth around 2:00 p.m. in the afternoon. The streets were clear of traffic, a good sign that the ski runs would also be clear. We went into the management office of the condo complex to check in. Bill asked the clerk for a calculator.

"Ok," Bill said to us, "the room is $169 per night, and we are staying four nights. That's $676, plus with room tax the total is $787.52. I already paid $250 for the deposit, so you each owe 1/3 of $787.52, which is $262.50, and you each owe me 1/3 of the deposit, which is $83.33."

Arguments between the men ensued, as Jim and John tried to convince Bill that his calculations were incorrect. Indeed, the way he had figured it, the three of us would be paying the entire bill, and he would be getting a free ride.

I stayed out of the fray, although the clerk and I shared some bemused looks between us. The arguments went on for about half an hour, and finally the men came to an agreement on the split. I paid what I was told to pay, but to this day I do not believe it was the correct amount.

After checking in, we unloaded the van. Immediately, Bill put the turkey into the oven. I had the single bedroom downstairs, and I became more uncomfortable when I realized the bedroom arrangement in the condo. The condo had one bedroom and a loft. The sitting room had a pullout bed. Bill informed me the three men would be sharing the loft. If I hadn't come along, they would not have had to share. One would have the bedroom, one the loft, and one the pullout bed in the sitting room. This made a far more logical arrangement, especially for John, who needed a hip replacement and found it difficult to climb stairs. I began to feel very out of place.

I unpacked, and then went to the kitchen. I made a fragrant tomato-based vegetable soup, adding in fresh tomatoes, butternut squash, fresh basil, and herbs de Provence. I poured in a little red wine to round it out. The soup had a certain sweetness to it from the vegetables. The fragrance was lovely, but the scent of roasting turkey overpowered the aroma.

I set the table, and ladled soup into the bowls. Bill carved the turkey. We sat down to eat and quickly the men fell silent and did not look up as they ate.

When the meal was just about done, Jim got up for seconds. "There's more turkey," Bill said. But Jim took seconds of the soup. As Jim sat down, John looked up and said, "Remember Peleliu?"

"And the wolf packs?" Bill said. "There were Germans all around us...wolf packs surrounding us. We knew they were there...couldn't hear them! Submarines all around. They were there...couldn't hear them, but we could feel them."

"Not until radar," John said. "Short wave...undetectable, the escort carriers...the high frequency direction finders. And hedgehogs."

They spoke in phrases, nodding in agreement with each other. I heard the words "Normandy," "88's," "Utah Beach," "U-boats," "Doenitz."

The conversation continued on as if I were no longer present. More accurately, they were no longer present at the dinner table in a condo in Mammoth. It was sixty years ago, and they were reliving the war.

I listened without interrupting. I enjoyed the history lesson, and I took it as an opportunity to hear firsthand from those who were there.

The next day, I awoke, dressed for skiing, and headed to the kitchen. I poured myself a cup of coffee. The men had already eaten breakfast, and Bill offered to serve me some "gruel." I looked into the pot on the stove. The pot was about 3 quarts in size, and the cereal filled the pot at least to the halfway point.

"We've already eaten, so you have to finish this," Bill said.

"Thank you, Bill," I said, "but I really can only eat just a little. I usually don't eat much for breakfast, just coffee and toast or fruit. That's way too much for me. I'm sorry but I can't finish all this."

"Well, you have to finish it. We've already eaten, and we can't waste it. It won't last overnight," Bill said.

I spooned a little of the gruel into a bowl and tasted it. I added a lot of sugar.

We were out the door quickly and at the lifts just before the mountain opened for skiing. It was a clear day, about 50 degrees, and the conditions were perfect.

For some reason, Bill had suddenly come to believe that I had never skied, and he wanted to give me lessons first. We started on some of the blue runs, and Bill gave me many excellent points. He seemed amazed at how quickly I was learning to ski.

Soon Bill and Jim went off to the black diamond runs, and I went with John to ski the intermediate runs. Since it was Monday, the mountain was nearly empty of people. With no lines at the lifts, we made countless runs...up to the summit, ski down to the lifts, over and over. In fact, all week the mountain was virtually empty, and not once did I stand in line at the lifts.

For most of the day, the beauty to the Sierras had the effect I desired. My anguished thoughts about the Navy subsided, and I focused on the serenity of the mountains.

That night for dinner, I made vegetable lasagna, and served some to all. Bill carved more meat from the day-old turkey. The men fell silent with their heads down as they ate their dinner. When Jim got up for seconds, Bill said, "There's more turkey." But Jim took more of the lasagna. As he sat down, John looked up and said, "Remember Peleliu?"

"And the wolf packs?" Bill said. "There were Germans all around us...wolf packs, surrounding us. We knew they were there...couldn't hear them! Submarines all around. They were there...couldn't hear them, but we could feel them."

"Not until radar," John said. short wave...undetectable, the escort carriers...the high frequency direction finders. And hedgehogs."

A sense of déjà vu swept over me. This was the same conversation verbatim as the night before. Again, the men were reliving the war. They knew their cues instinctively, who would say what and when. This scene repeated itself each night for the entire week. Jim went for second helpings, and John began with "Remember Peleliu?"

These men spoke quietly showing little emotion. However, as I listened closely, I began to sense the dread and speechless terror they had felt while surrounded by a silent invisible evil, the German wolf packs. I began to sense the rituals that pulled them back to war each night. But I also sensed that in these rituals established over the decades that they had found acknowledgement and confirmation that their fears had not been exaggerated, reassurances only they could give to each other. The evil had been real.

That night as I lay in bed, my mind wandered back to my job at the Navy. I tried to refocus on the day, the peaceful snowy slopes, and the feelings of sailing unencumbered down the mountain. Yet I could not silence the broken record. I kept replaying in my mind this episode or that conversation. I agonized over what I could have done differently, if anything.

In addition to the thoughts about the Navy, my mind drifted back against my will to the sexual abuse in my childhood. Initially, I would recall one or two incidents, then as time passed that year, those memories became like the broken record of memories of sexual harassment. I also wondered if I would ever have someone with whom I could share the experience of sexual abuse. Just as the men had each other to share about the war, I wanted someone to share with me, to acknowledge the evil had been real.

I considered broaching the subject once again to Gretchen. However, I had clearly erred in Nepal by hurling the topic at her without warning and out of anger and indignation. It gave her the opportunity to go on the defensive and intentionally disregard my pain. In short, I had played my hand badly.

However early that same year, the news headlines offered a breach in the brick wall. The Boston Globe broke the story of extensive sexual abuse committed by priests in the Catholic Church. This news cracked open the door to the dark world of pedophile priests hiding themselves behind clerical collars as well as Bishops and Cardinals exposed for refusing to defrock the criminal priests or at least report them to law enforcement. Rather, Cardinal Bernard Law of the Catholic Archdiocese of Boston covered up the credible accusations for years, even decades. The initial coverage focused on five specific priests, although ultimately the investigation led to subsequent investigations and more credible allegations. In early 2002, it appeared to be isolated to Boston, not the global crisis it was destined to become.

I began to wonder about Gretchen. I wanted to talk to her, but I already knew that anything less than shining acclaim regarding Konrad drew a sharp reprimand from her. The brief, painful discussion in Nepal had me convinced that she would not respond well if I addressed the issue of sexual abuse with her. Still, the issue of incest had to be brought out into the light, and I began making plans to initiate a conversation on a level less fraught with tortuous memories and painful emotions.

The next morning, I was the last to the kitchen for breakfast. A four-quart stock pot simmered on the stove.

"There's plenty of gruel left over for you, Wendy," Bill said. "You will have to finish it for us."

I looked inside the pot, which was bigger than the pot from the day before. Again, the brown, sticky gruel filled the pot to at least the halfway mark. I couldn't possibly finish the leftover amount, let alone put a significant dent into it. I wanted only a cup of coffee, yet I spooned a small amount of the hot cereal into a bowl and ate it.

I said nothing to Bill about this. I knew he would be upset about wasting so much food. Yet, he was responsible for making so much. I watched his frustrated expression as he poured the leftovers down the sink to clean the pot. It was a sad waste of food.

We headed off to the lifts, and again I skied with John. My mind cleared almost instantly, and I could feel my nerves relax. The mountains may not have this effect on all people, but for me, I have always been able to live in the moment when there.

Moment by moment, the glorious sights, the fragrant pines, and the peaceful sounds guided my thoughts through my senses. I forgot all about the Navy while gliding down the slopes.

That night at dinner, the talk among the men turned to the war again.

Throughout the whole week, the trip had a certain feeling of déjà vu. Each morning we ate gruel, and the amounts of gruel, which Bill made, became increasingly greater. Each evening, the men ate the aging turkey and talked about the war. Sometimes I felt as though my presence was inconsequential to the unspoken rules and rituals, as the men abided by them out of habit. And sometimes I felt I had intruded on something excruciatingly personal.

And each night as I went to bed, I fell into my own ritual, replaying the memories of my time working at the Navy in my mind, although I fought it as best I could. Over the years to come, I came to believe that watching the men fall into their conversations of the war acted as a trigger to replay my memories of a difficult time, and those memories acted as a trigger for deeper memories. However, what I went through at the Navy was insignificant compared to what these WWII vets had endured. Eventually, the broken record regarding the sexual harassment stopped playing in my mind. Yet, the broken record about sexual abuse was about to replace that other scratched vinyl.

I had some humorous moments skiing with John. He was my "designated partner" in skiing, since neither one of us wished to take on the moguls or black diamond runs. I liked John very much. He was very friendly and a gentleman. He tried hard to relate to me. And he tried very hard to get me to open up. Yet he respected my space as well.

In retrospect, I regret not being able to open up to him. My stress levels were continuing to increase although I didn't fully recognize it at the time. Besides I think he truly enjoyed being seen on the slopes with some "young chick."

On day three, John convinced me to try a very short black diamond run that extends from the Knee Deep run and lies between the Stump Alley and Old Comeback runs, which are both blue squares.

I took the switchbacks very slowly, and I felt gravity pulling strongly as soon as I pointed my ski tips downhill to make the turn. Perhaps my caution in the turns caused the mishap or not. But about halfway down the run, I fell forward down the slope. I was making an upside-down snow angel, with my head pointed downhill, and my legs flailing ungracefully behind me at ridiculous angles. I was so glad no one got photos. Every tiny movement I made to right myself resulted in the beginning of an uncontrolled slide down the slope. Poor John with his bad hip was already at the bottom of the run, yet he climbed up the slope to help me stand upright. Then we skied down together.

On the last day of skiing, I had gone off on my own to ski alone for a while. I told John I would meet him back at the van. I made it back to the parking lot before he did. I got in the van, and thinking no one was around, I took off my top to take off my sports bra. I was briefly topless. As I pulled my top back on, out of the corner of my eye, I caught sight of John looking in the window of the van. It was one of those "Kodak" moments. I knew that he knew that I knew. He knew that I knew that he knew. Yet nothing was ever said. He got a full-frontal flash.

After I got past my initial discomfort, I began to sense a small link to their experiences, experiences that we all should remember in the hopes of preventing future wars. And I felt a link to them while they tried to make sense of a trauma which defies words.

Perhaps these three men saw their annual jaunts to Mammoth as nothing more than ski trips. Yet, I sensed something deeper. They gathered each year for a remembrance of their experience in the war under the guise of a ski trip. I felt honored by the invitation; in forty years, this was the only time they let in an outsider.

We returned home that Friday. By that time, I had the whole "kitty" issue resolved and the drive home was uneventful. As I unpacked my duffel bag at home, I knew that any time I made my way up to Mammoth to go skiing, I would remember their remembrances.

10

Valentine's Day on Villager Peak - February 2002

As I settled into life on La Cresta Drive, I realized that Julie's house was almost exclusively mine during the school year. She and her companion, Bob, both worked high up in an organization dedicated to helping disadvantaged youth get into college. Her job had her traveling for weeks at a time. She would pack two to three suitcases in advance. Then, she left early on Sundays with one suitcase and returned late on Saturday night. Early the next day, she would grab the next suitcase and head out again. When she was finally home for a week, she did mountains of laundry.

Bob traveled as well, but not quite as much as Julie. He was a quiet, caring, and compassionate individual while Julie was also caring and compassionate. And, her first comments to me about him were true. He frequently went straight up to the master bedroom using the back paths to the top of the property.

However, I could never characterize Julie as a quiet soul. She wasn't loud or anxious; her cheerful spirit flooded entire rooms as she entered. Bright and vivacious, Julie was someone I came to admire even though I saw her rarely. When I did run into her as she was coming or going, she would assure me that summers were different. Then the schools took their breaks, and her work would quiet down until fall.

So, I had this amazing home and plenty of space to reorient myself to life in Point Loma. Julie's home held many surprises though. She hired a housekeeper several times per month to clean, and her home was stunning. Still, when I opened cabinets in the kitchen, they were cluttered and dirty. I couldn't understand why she didn't hire the housekeeper once or twice to clean the cabinets as well. So, little by little, I began to pull out their contents and clean the interiors. One day, I went into the kitchen to make my morning coffee, and my cat, Skittles, was crouching and focused on the refrigerator. I knew this hunting stance well, so I moved the refrigerator out enough for her to get behind it. Within a couple of days, she had brought me several dead mice as gifts.

Plus, Julie had clearly made a large investment in remodeling her home. However, she hadn't touched the original two bedrooms and bathroom that she rented out. The bathroom had the original pink tiling that was so popular in the 1950s and the original bathtub and fixtures.

One Friday after the ski trip, I was at Bill and Ginny's kitchen counter when Julie came bounding in. She had returned a day early, dropped off her suitcase, then headed over to catch up with them. Bob joined in as well. As always, the conversation turned to politics, and I was the sole conservative. Still the discussions were always polite. Julie and Ginny had been the best of friends ever since Julie moved in next door as a young bride thirty years prior.

I found a job, which was a relief. It was on the nearby Marine base, and eventually I learned that gossip travels quickly in the military. Everything that had happened to me at the Navy base followed me to my new position. There was no harassment, but the vicious gossip began to pervade my daily life. I couldn't escape it at work, which meant I would need to find a new career.

My relationship with Werner was flourishing. For the first time ever, I felt I had found family with him and Bill and Ginny and Bob and Julie. I felt a little disloyal to my dad, but not to Gretchen. Bill and Ginny were so accepting and positive. Ginny would frequently tell me how pretty I was or compliment my beautiful hair. I had never had a mother figure say those things to me. I was at their kitchen counter several times a week, and that was how I eventually met the entire neighborhood. Everyone stopped by, walked in without knocking, and had a cocktail with Bill and Ginny.

Werner and I both enjoyed hiking, although I learned later that Werner was a world class mountaineer having climbed some of the biggest mountains in the world: Aconcagua, McKinley, Gasherbrum, among others. His brash talk about Mount Everest being a walk up began to seem reasonable considering his abilities. I thought it was a big deal to climb in the Sierras in California, where the tallest mountain, Mount Whitney, is just over 14,000'.

Eventually, I became keenly aware of the differences in our climbing abilities. However, while love was new, Werner suggested an overnight campout on Villager Peak in Anza Borrego Desert State Park for Valentine's Day.

Villager is located on the opposite side of Anza Borrego from Oriflamme, where I had encountered my spirit coyote while camping at the oasis. The view from the peak includes a panorama of the Salton Sea to the east, Borrego Valley to the southwest, and Rabbit peak to the north.

This was an unusual idea for celebrating Valentines, but I was charmed and amused. And in honesty, I think I wanted to impress him with my hiking abilities.

We left San Diego around 4:00 a.m., and arrived in Anza Borrego about 5:30 a.m. We were equipped and hiking by 6:00 a.m. To reach the base of the ridge, we crossed Rattlesnake Canyon Wash, which can best be described as a maze of gullies crisscrossing each other. We reached the base around 6:45 a.m. and started on the old Indian trail up the ridgeline.

Villager was spectacularly beautiful. However, we could not enjoy the scenery, let alone see what was around us. When we left that morning, the sky was overcast, which in the desert most often denotes good climbing weather. The clouds did not seem to be storm clouds. Yet, as we continued with the hike, the sky darkened swiftly, and the temperature dropped sharply. Soon we were in a heavy fog, so heavy that I couldn't see my feet or the trail. Rain began to fall in the early afternoon, yet we had gone too far to turn back. We continued on.

My equipment, backpack, and clothing were not waterproofed, or even water resistant. By the time we reached the peak, I was soaked through and freezing. My fingers were numb, and I couldn't help Werner with pitching the tent. I sat under a pinyon pine trying to avoid more rain.

Once the tent was pitched, I got in. Werner climbed in after me. My shivering grew more obvious, and I sat quietly in the corner of the tent. Werner unpacked his backpack, and his clothes and sleeping bag were dry. He insisted that I take off my wet clothes and put on his dry ones. I gratefully complied with one exception. I declined the balaclava as it would make me feel claustrophobic.

Then Werner insisted that I take his dry sleeping bag. I got in and waited for the inside of the bag to warm up.

He brought out his MSR pocket rocket and boiled a small pot of water. I don't recall what we had to eat, other than it was a pasta meal in a "make it in the packet" foil container. It tasted fabulous. I think we had hot cocoa for dessert.

Werner took my wet sleeping bag, and I am sure he was freezing all night. Nevertheless, he took care of me, and I was warm.

I am not much of a complainer, although I am sure other women (yes, even some men!) would have whined and moaned. So, I didn't complain about the cold or rain. To do so would have changed nothing. I could have checked the weather report prior to our trip, yet I don't recall that rain was forecasted anyway. It was just bad luck. It wasn't anyone's fault.

We broke camp in the morning. The clouds had disappeared, and the sun was shining. We had coffee, then we headed down the mountain. After the rain and in the glorious sunlight, the beauty of the desert mountain was spectacular. However, the hard hike the previous day had worn me out, plus my knees have always had more difficulty hiking down a trail. I started to feel the pain, and that slowed me down a bit. We finally reached the car after several hours of hiking down and on the way back to San Diego, we stopped at Carlee's for lunch.

In retrospect, that hike in the storm was a portent of the hard hikes and raging storms still to face me in 2002. However, on that particular mountain and in that particular storm, I had Werner caring and watching out for me, and that made all the difference.

After I got home and unpacked, I tried calling John Havens, but his phone rang with no answer even though I let it ring 25 to 30 times. I kept trying every few days. But, one day I tried calling him, and I got the standard phone company message that the call could not be completed as dialed. I tried emailing him. I received an automated message from the system administrator that said, "Your message was undeliverable."

John passed away at the age of fifty from brain cancer.

A friend of his emailed me once or twice while she tried to keep Oxventure alive. It was not to be. Later, Steve Webster of Escape2Nepal carried on John's ideas of helping the disabled reach the top summits of the world.

John climbed his final mountain never to descend. I still had mountains to climb and stories to write. I didn't know it then, but I was facing several years of climbing metaphorical mountains, even as I headed to the backcountry for some real mountain climbing with Werner.

11

Easter at Gretchen's - March 31, 2002

By 2002, much of my extended family from my mother's side had scattered away from the Southern California region. Some went to Northern California, some to the Northwest, some to the Dakotas. Some family from my father's side lived still in Southern California. Easter was approaching at the end of March, and typically we didn't celebrate the holiday with them.

Gretchen planned a small Easter meal including Lynne, her second husband, Mike, my nephew, and me. I invited Werner as a chance to meet some of my family. It was a little early in our relationship to introduce him to family, but I rarely saw my mother after my father's death. He said he would consider it and took my mother's address. At the last moment, he declined to come along. Since he wasn't attending and I typically saw Gretchen only on a few holidays, I decided to seek out an opportunity to discuss the growing sexual abuse scandal with the Catholic Church to lead into initiating a conversation on the subject of sexual abuse in our own family.

Lynne had already been there for several hours when I arrived. As usual, she and Gretchen were glued to each other and cooking dinner together in the kitchen. They shared private stories and laughed to themselves as they prepared the meal.

Gretchen had also invited two men who were a couple and had no family nearby to enjoy a nice holiday. They were both very congenial, and I joined them in the family room to socialize over appetizers.

Gretchen planned a formal dinner in the dining room, and she prepared a whole salmon stuffed with fennel, seasoned with thyme and splashed with a touch of orange juice. Ina Garten created the recipe, and her trick to a moist salmon included baking it at 500 degrees for exactly 30 minutes, not more, not less; a point that Gretchen repeated to everyone as she entertained from the kitchen.

I headed to the dining room to set the table, fill the water glasses, and light the candles. These were my usual duties for a formal meal. Gretchen always insisted on the correct place settings with the utensils placed in the order of use from the outside in as usual. Salad plates rested to the left of the dinner plate, and beverage glasses rested to the right. I put the wine glasses on the inside of the setting and the water glasses on the outside.

As I began filling the water glasses, she came in. Immediately she began berating me for setting the glasses incorrectly.

"Oh, oh! No, you set them wrong. The water glass goes on the inside. How could you do that. It's totally wrong. I didn't teach you that way! Oh, oh!"

She was being overly melodramatic considering how easy it was to fix the placement of the glasses. But she acted as if I had committed a capital offense. I had seen her this way before, and I wondered if she had taken up drinking again.

I circled the dining room table to reset the water and wine glasses. As I did, I casually mentioned the headlines.

"I've been following the news about the Catholic Church in Boston. Have you read about it? Read how they knew that five of the priests were child molesters. The hierarchy knew, but they kept transferring the priests around, so they just kept on molesting children and getting away with it. I think it's terrible."

Gretchen didn't look at me. Instead she also circled the dining table and made multiple, minute adjustments to the settings by moving plates and glasses closer together or further apart. These were diversionary moves as she really didn't change the settings.

I continued. "Most Americans are shocked that this could happen in a church. No one expected that a child molester would actually become a priest and use his position to hide his crimes. But, it's true. It's coming out."

Gretchen moved the forks slightly at the setting at the head of the table further demonstrating how horribly I had set the table according to her standards.

"It's not possible. Those children are obviously mentally ill. Someone is planting false memories into them. They're being hypnotized. The children are sick. No priest or pastor would ever do such a thing. They're mentally ill," she said.

"Look, I've been reading some of the accounts," I said. "These are adults coming forward saying they were sexually abused by these priests as children. No one has been hypnotized, and no one is mentally ill. The evidence is there. The Catholic Church knew what was going on and transferred these monsters around. They should have called the police instead."

"You're wrong. It's a witch hunt. The children are all sick, mentally ill," she declared.

My idea of opening the topic obviously failed. However, I learned very clearly from that encounter what her denials would entail if I continued on with speaking up about sexual abuse in our family. There was no doubt in my mind that she knew exactly where I was going with the conversation, especially considering the conversation we had in Nepal. Now I knew that if I spoke out against Konrad, she would use his tactics and label me as mentally ill and cut me off. I had to consider very carefully how to move forward with speaking the truth.

I switched subjects and shared some other news. I had written to the adoption agency that placed me with my family and asked for any information they had on my biological parents. Werner had encouraged me to do this.

As I told my mother about the information from the adoption agency, I wasn't sure how she would react. I hoped she would be happy for me.

"Did they tell you anything?" she asked.

"Yes, it was all non-identifying; however, they gave me almost three pages of information," I said. "Apparently, my bio mom left a lot of genealogical data with occupations of parents and grandparents. She and my bio dad were both seventeen, so it sounded like a high school fling. Her father was a dentist, and her paternal grandfather was a colonel in the Marines. She left a lot of health information too. Her family on both sides was English and Welsh, but she referred to my bio dad as 'black Irish.'"

"They didn't give us any information when we adopted your brother," she said.

This left me confused. Did the agency give her the same information it gave me, but she withheld it from me all these years?

As a teenager, my brother got into trouble with the law on several occasions, although he eventually straightened out his life.

"They didn't tell us anything. They just dropped him off. I think they were hiding that he was a drug baby. The mother was a drug addict. They gave us a defective baby," she said.

As she said those words, it seemed to me that her voice changed. When she spoke that final phrase, "They gave us a defective baby," I heard Konrad's baritone voice instead of hers.

Her comment stunned me. Just several years prior on the trip to Nepal, I had addressed the issue that her father had referred to adopted kids as defective. He said it right to my face, although later he said, "I didn't mean you."

Too late. Gretchen repeated the words to me that day on Easter. She didn't retract her words either or even seem to understand how hurtful the comment was to me. I stood speechless wondering what move to make. This was strike two for me.

The doorbell rang, and Lynne went to answer the door. Werner walked in with flowers for my mother. He had changed his mind and driven up to have dinner and meet family. After introductions, Lynne and Gretchen quietly set out an extra place setting on the dining table. Dinner was ready, and we all sat down to eat.

The salmon made an impressive entrée, and we all admired it for a moment after saying grace and before Gretchen began serving it. She went into minute details about how to prepare it—just a splash of orange juice, just a splash. And cook it for exactly 30 minutes at 500 degrees.

Indeed, Gretchen always had a flair for lovely dinner settings, exquisite platings, and very delicious food. When my father was alive, we ate our meals around what he liked, because type 1 diabetics need to control their diets very carefully. My dad liked things very plain. Meat, chicken, potatoes, peas, beans, and corn. Salad was iceberg lettuce and sliced tomato–no dressing. After he passed away, Gretchen enjoyed diving deeply into much more exotic, flavorful fare.

Werner was always sociable, and we had a good meal. He gave Gretchen a bit of information: he was a senior geologist for the city of San Diego, he liked rock climbing, mountain climbing, kayaking. He had two grown daughters.

The conversation around the table was convivial, and Gretchen refilled her wine glass several times through the meal. She began to dominate the discussion and turned her focus more to Werner and asked him several highly personal questions. He deflected those questions with a bit of humor.

However, while I was polite, my mind focused on Gretchen's words to me before dinner. This was the moment I seriously began questioning God and why he included honoring your father and mother in the Ten Commandments. She cared more about protecting her appearance of perfection rather than caring if I was hurting. All I saw was a woman who couldn't acknowledge or even understand how wounding her words were.

After the meal, I helped bring dirty dishes into the kitchen for washing. I noticed Gretchen pull Werner aside. She was talking intently to him. Already, I knew Werner and his personality well. He smiled and nodded, but given his upbringing, he was very savvy about people. That savviness was showing in his expression. Gretchen touched his elbow while saying a few final words, then she went into the living room.

Werner and I left together, but we headed to our respective cars. When we were out of earshot of the others, he stopped me.

"Your mother has issues, doesn't she?" he asked.

"Yeah, why, what did she say to you in there?"

"She warned me that you are mentally ill and told me to stay away from you. She wanted me to keep it as 'our little secret.' She said she took your history and letters to a psychiatrist and had you diagnosed with borderline personality disorder."

"Really? Did she give you the name of that psychiatrist, because I guarantee that I've never met him. That would be highly unethical for a doctor to diagnose someone without ever meeting that person," I said.

"I don't believe her. I'm just letting you know. Does she always do this to you? It's pretty mean for a mother. Is she intentionally trying to drive me away?" he asked.

"I don't know. She and I are not close. I usually stay away from her and only do the major holidays."

"Well, I'm sure she loves you in her own way," he offered.

"I doubt that," I replied.

"Anyway, a few of us are climbing San Jacinto this coming Saturday. Do you want to come?" he asked.

"I'll be there. I've hiked Mount San Jacinto many times," I replied.

"Good, be at my house by 11:30 p.m. We leave at midnight exactly, and we will be on the trail by 3:00 a.m. Don't be late. And if you don't have a headlamp, bring a flashlight," he said. Then we both drove home in our respective cars.

That was the day Gretchen began her insidious smear campaign against me. Prior to that day, we had a poor relationship at best. Now she waged an all-out war against me. I was officially on her hit list.

She called family and close friends and told them the same thing she told Werner. She pulled a mythical doctor out of her hat. When I broached the subject of pedophile ministers, she went on the defense with an aggressive offense.

Many family members and friends called me to warn me what she was saying about me. As with Werner, she would finish by saying to keep it their little secret. It was no secret, although she may not have known that so many people were divulging what she said.

As the sexual abuse scandal in the Catholic Church exploded, and as she now had a clear notion that my intent was to talk about sexual abuse in our family, her war against me exploded as well. The interactions that day convinced me she knew her father was a pedophile, but for some bizarre reason, she would defend him with rigid, unrelenting allegiance. She would defend by attacking.

Gretchen had many fine qualities, but this is one aspect of her personality that I disliked immensely. Any conflict with a person led her denigrate that individual mercilessly. The slander never ceased, and I was now a target of her disparagement.

I began to pull away and visit her less and less.

12

Climbing Snow Creek - April 2002

Later that week, I touched base with Werner about the climb up Mount San Jacinto to find out who was climbing and what time we would leave.

Werner and several of his friends, David, Mark, and Andreas, were planning a trip to Nepal to climb Ama Dablam, a 23,000-foot peak just south of Mount Everest and renowned for the technical ice climbing required to summit the peak.

The entire group of friends and a few others had planned a hike up Snow Creek for training. Snow Creek is a 10,000' rise on the north face of Mount San Jacinto, which is famous for the little tourist town of Idyllwild on one side, and the tram from Palm Springs on the other.

Mount San Jacinto stands at 10,500', far less than the 14,000' peaks I had climbed in the Sierras. I had been to the summit of Mount San Jacinto many times using the Devil's Slide trail from Idyllwild. Werner described Snow Creek as "a day hike," but also as an "ass kicker." I was unfazed. I used Mount San Jacinto for training hikes in preparation for high altitude work in the Sierras as well. The mountain was like an outdoor playground to me.

I was lacking crampons and an ice ax, so Werner came over and took me to Bill's house next door to borrow some equipment. Age had not dulled the sharpness of mind for either Bill or Ginny, but something affected Bill's ability to verbalize his thoughts. Occasionally the flow of words stopped. His thoughts were there and his frustration grew as he struggled to speak.

However, some tension arose when Werner indicated the climbing gear was for me, and we would be climbing Snow Creek. Bill's face clearly expressed deep concern, but the words did not flow easily from his mouth.

"You can't...not...take her...up...Snow Creek!" Bill exclaimed.

Werner did not respond. In retrospect, this was the first installment of a lesson I learned about Werner, although I did not realize it at the time. His strength and athletic skills were far superior to anyone else. If something was an ass-kicker to him, it could put the average person in the hospital. On the way out, Werner told me that Bill's memory was not the same since a climbing accident he had several years prior.

On the day of the climb, we left San Diego precisely at midnight. Once we arrived at the tiny community of Snow Creek, we unloaded the cars, settled our packs with the gear and supplies, and began hiking by 3:00 a.m. Werner was in the lead.

I had been sure about my abilities, but only five minutes into the hike, I knew I was out of my league. The pace was fast. I had only a flashlight, which was inadequate to the situation. I wore only low-topped approach shoes with no support, and I stumbled easily, twisting my ankles frequently.

The others had headlamps flooding the way before them with fluorescent light. The first leg of the climb was not technically difficult, but I was unaccustomed to hiking in the dark. I fell behind quickly, and I found my way only by following the headlamps flickering in the distance like a line of fireflies.

We stopped for a rest at around 5:30 a.m. The darkness hid the shadowy outline of the mountain, preventing me from orienting myself. Werner sat beside me and offered me some of his orange juice.

"When we get to about 5500 feet, we'll stop for another break. We'll be at the lower edge of the couloir and the snow. You'll put on our boots and crampons. Then I will show you several techniques for climbing, especially how to stop yourself with your ice ax if you fall. We stick together to prevent falls. But if you fall, the only one who can save you is you," Werner said.

We started up the trail again, and the incline changed significantly, becoming much steeper. The pale light of dawn arrived adding to the sureness of my steps. We were in an extremely narrow chasm with huge granite walls that blocked any view of the mountain peak above and the desert floor below. We gained elevation swiftly, and the trail included some bouldering. Again, I was the caboose, and I fell so far behind I could not see or hear the group.

A staggering wall of huge boulders stretching across the entire chasm stopped me dead in my tracks. Obviously, there was no other way to go. I struggled for several minutes to find an initial hand hold, and then shimmied my way up the cracks between the boulders. Several times, I resorted to the very ungraceful, and frowned upon, technique of using my knees.

I could hear voices laughing and talking as I pulled myself over the lip of the last boulder. As I did, the laughing turned to cheering. We were finally at the edge of the snow tongue and the beginning of the real climb.

I sat down facing away from the mountain to catch my breath. I pulled out a PowerBar and water from my pack for breakfast although the exertion had diminished my appetite. I turned around for a first look at the climb ahead, and the sight took my breath away.

The mountain rose 5,000 feet from our site at what seemed to be a nearly vertical rise. Later, I learned the angle was only 35 degrees at most. However, it did not matter. This was more than I had anticipated. For the first time, I realized that hardcore mountaineers do not look for the quickest way, or the simplest way, or the prettiest and most pleasant way to the summit of a peak. They deliberately choose the most difficult route up a mountain and then make a race of it.

Once I was outfitted with boots, crampons, and the ice ax, Werner gave me brief instructions in front pointing and the French technique of standing flat footed to climb. He demonstrated the correct grasp of the ice axe for the self-arrest position, with the thumb under the adze, and the palm and fingers over the pick near the shaft. Self-arrest is the most effective recovery measure from an uncontrollable fall, and the most desirable position for self-arrest is head uphill, facing sideways. The climber jabs the axe into the ice and hopefully stops the fall.

We began the climb up the couloir. Very quickly, the group fell into rhythm. Steve took the lead cutting switchbacks in the snow, and the other climbers followed his footsteps. I was no longer last in line, since Werner was directly behind me bringing up the rear. However, the group ahead climbed at a much greater speed than I did, and as such both Werner and I fell behind. As we gained elevation, my heart was racing and my breathing was shallow and fast. I stopped every fourth or fifth switchback to catch my breath.

"What are you, my private Sherpa? Why don't you go on ahead? I'm just holding you back. I can follow the tracks myself," I said to Werner.

"No. This is good," he said.

The group stopped for lunch at about 7500 feet. Werner, David, and I sat together on a rock. I had a cheese sandwich, but I could not tolerate the thought of a bite or even a sip of water. Waves of nausea from the physical exertion roiled over me. David noticed I was not eating, and he gently insisted that I try.

Werner's attention was focused on his brother-in-law, John, as he crossed the couloir and inspected a large bush on the other side. John looked morose as he kicked around in the ice as if he was searching for something buried.

Werner finally turned away to eat his lunch.

"This is the first trip up Snow Creek for any of us since Bill's accident. John and Bill were climbing this alone five years ago. Bill was behind John when he slipped and fell almost 1000' down the ice before he stopped. He was badly injured and unconscious, and that's the bush John secured him to while he went down the mountain for help. They had to send in a Huey from El Toro Marine Base to pick him up off the mountain. He almost died," Werner explained.

"This is where Bill had his climbing accident? And he was climbing this at his age?" I asked.

"Yes, he's strong, and he's climbed this mountain more than any of us combined, but I should have gone along," Werner answered.

"Am I wearing the gear he was using?" I asked. Werner did not reply.

After resting for about thirty minutes, we began climbing again. The summit was soon less than 1000' feet above us. I have never struggled so hard with any climb, even those at higher altitudes. I stopped at every turn in the switchbacks to breathe; my heart raced at the speed of light, and with each beat it came up through my throat. My head pounded with a throbbing pain that seemed to split me in two. My vision became blurred, and every muscle screamed in pain. I could feel the skin on my right heel rubbing off from the friction of the boot. I thought about turning around, but one look down the mountain convinced me that going up was the only option.

Again, I suggested to Werner that he go ahead of me. Again, he said no.

I barely reached the saddle of the chute we were climbing. The rest of the group turned right to finish hiking to the top, but I could not join them. As I waited for them to come back, I looked up at the peak and felt the deadening sense of defeat grip me.

How could this mountain, this playground, conquer me, crush me? The answer from the mountain came to me like a soft whisper in my mind. "You underestimated me. You did not know this side of me existed," the mountain told me.

The group came down from the peak, and we started for the second half of the climb, the descent. However, we did not climb down Snow Creek. We continued over the saddle to the other side of the mountain, hiked across Round Valley several miles to the lodge, and caught the tram down to Palm Springs. With the danger of slipping down the ice on Snow Creek gone, Werner took off at his own speed again. I was hiking alone, although I knew my way. I was beyond exhaustion, and several times I fell forward onto my knees retching with dry heaves. I reached the lodge at 4:00 p.m., fully thirteen hours of climbing. Once there, I removed my boots, and my right sock was soaked with blood.

Someone in the group hailed a taxi van. Once it arrived, we had the driver take us to the little town of Snow Creek to pick up the cars, and we headed home. It took me days to recover from the climb, and for once, I didn't find any peace and serenity from hiking in the mountains. I found no relief from the escalating anxiety and fear I felt fueled by what happened at the Navy, the satellite photo letter, the headlines about pedophile priests, and Gretchen's smear campaign.

13

Canon Tajo – Summer 2002

A few weeks later, Werner and his buddies took off for four weeks to travel to Nepal and climb Ama Dablam. When he returned, we continued dating. Eventually, he took me to a place in Baja where he and his rock climbing friends would visit called Canon Tajo. It is internationally famous among rock climbers because the mountains there have a dome that is bigger than Half Dome in Yosemite. Called El Gran Trono Blanco, the Great White Dome, the routes are typically around twelve pitches. The most famous routes are Giraffe and Pan-American. Werner and his buddy, Mark, built a route called Leaving on a Jet Plane, and most of the routes are rated 5.14 and above.

However, getting to the dome is extremely difficult, and many climbers who know where it is keep it a secret. For many years, they would intentionally post warnings on the internet about harassment by the Federales or robberies by banditos. The directions to get there go something like this: when you see the empty beer bottle hanging from the tree, turn right. When you get to the fork in the dirt road that has a boulder in the middle, take the left fork. But first you need to find the mesa at the top of the escarpment, which is an extension of the Laguna mountains in San Diego.

Werner and I would leave at 4:00 a.m. on Saturday mornings for the two hour drive. At the time, the border crossing at Tecate was lightly used and crossings went very quickly. Then we would drive east on the toll road until we reached a small town, exit, and head south on the dirt roads.

Canon Tajo is an altitude of about 5,000 feet with many pinyon pines. It is on top of the Sierra Juarez section of the Laguna Mountains, but an ancient Indian trail on the north side heads down into the canyon itself. A creek runs through the canyon with blue palms along the banks for plenty of shade. It is from that vantage point that visitors can see the dome. However, to approach the dome from the floor of Laguna Salada is at least a six-day hike with no fresh water along the way until you reach that creek. The only real approach is to hike from the mesa alongside the side of the massive dome. Since a climb of the dome is one to two days with nights spent on a portaledge on the rock, climbers typically make two to three trips to take all of their gear to the beginning of the actual climb.

That type of climbing was way beyond anything I could do. 5.7 or 5.8 was the highest level I attempted, and I personally didn't get any enjoyment out of it. Still, Werner and I went down to Canon Tajo at least two to three weekends of every month and hiked around the mesa and granite outcroppings.

One weekend, he turned right rather than left on the dirt road to go exploring. He knew of a cattle ranch near the campsite and wanted to check it out. We drove up to the fence and gate of Rancho El Topo. I got out to open the gate, which wasn't locked. Just inside was a tattered barn, some corrals, and small home. The area has no electricity or running water, and this ranch had only one well. Werner parked the car adjacent to the corrals, and we got out.

Soon, an older gentleman came out of the home and approached us. Werner knew no Spanish, and this gentleman knew no English. They had never met, but somehow they communicated with each other very well. Werner wanted to ride a horse, and Señor Sandoval said, "Si." Soon, he had two horses saddled, which we rode while Señor Sandoval rode one of his burros. He took us on a brief ride and showed us the creek running through his property and several trails that lead to old abandoned gold mines.

When we came back to the barn, Werner offered him some money for the ride, which Señor Sandoval graciously accepted. Then we headed to the campground.

The next weekend, we pulled off the toll road just before getting to La Rumorosa and purchased several bales of hay. We skipped the campground and headed straight for Rancho El Topo. We donated the hay to Señor Sandoval, saddled up horses again, and took off on a long ride. That soon became our usual destination rather than the climbing area. It wasn't long before other climbing friends came along.

After some bargaining, Señor Sandoval went out during the week and shopped for horses for us. We bought our own horses through him and left them there in his care for a small monthly fee that was very inexpensive. It was a win/win. He had more horses to use during cattle roundups and income from us to take care of them. Plus, we always brought in more hay and feed for all of the horses.

These were glorious days. In fact, these were the only small moments of peace in that year of escalating fear and anxiety. Being around Señor Sandoval was calming to me. He was a true horse whisperer. His horses loved him, and he knew them well. They were all beautiful and well trained. My horse was huge standing taller than 17 hands. He was a Palomino: tall, blond and handsome, so his name became Hollywood. Werner had a dark, spirited bay named

Hidalgo. We spent our days riding around the land, and one of our favorite trails took us past the campground and to the top of a lookout. From there, we could see into the deep canyon and catch a glimpse of El Gran Trono Blanco.

We began to camp out on the ranch itself. Set off away from the Sandoval's home, there was a little area with a good view of the granite escarpment. One weekend, Werner brought something in a small box with us. Once we set up the tent, he took an urn out of the box. It was his mother's ashes, he told me. He brought them along to place them among the serene landscape.

"I think this is a good place for Helga to be," he said.

"It's certainly a beautiful place. Didn't you once tell me that it was Bill who first discovered Canon Tajo and started climbing here? Did you all come down here with him? Did Helga ever see this place?" I asked.

"No. I just think this is a peaceful place for her" came his reply.

We started off on a hike and came across a small outcropping of boulders. We climbed to the top and placed Helga's urn into a crevice beneath the stones. Werner was pensive when he said, "Helga is finally at rest." He said something in German, then we went back to the barn and saddled up Hollywood and Hidalgo for a long ride.

That night as we sat around a campfire staring at the billions of stars in the sky, Werner opened up a little more about Helga. His stepfather had been physically abusive to her. He drank heavily and flew into rages. Werner filled the role of protector more than once. He faced more abuse out on the streets of the Bronx. No on protected him; he learned the hard way to defend himself.

"My stepfather was a real S.O.B. Once when I was just out of the Marines, I was looking for a job and had no money for food. So, I called him and asked if I could borrow $20 for groceries. Bastard said no."

We were quiet for a little while. Then, he said something out of the blue:

"Helga should never have been a mother."

I was surprised. I hadn't heard him say anything disloyal about her. Indeed, I never realized until that moment a person could say something disloyal about a parent. He never told me why he said it. He never told me what she had done to earn that disloyalty so many years after her death, and I was certain that I was the only person to ever hear him criticize Helga.

We had some things in common that many people will never understand. Our mothers didn't protect us even though that's what mothers are supposed to do. Maybe Werner knew enough of Helga's history to know why she couldn't safeguard him, but he didn't venture to say. However, I eventually came to a conclusion myself about my mother and her inability to protect me, although it was many years later.

14

East to West – July 2002

In late July, Julie made plans to have the wood floors in her home refinished. This meant vacating her home for at least three days while the workers completed the sanding, varnishing, and polishing. All the furniture needed to be removed from the home as well, and my cat needed to be sheltered. Julie approached me about taking that time to do some hiking in the backcountry while the work took place during the renovations. Although in her late 50s, Julie was very fit, and I knew she had taken many trips to the Sierras. I agreed it was a fine idea.

She said she wanted to traverse the Sierras. I had hiked from Mammoth to Yosemite several years prior, so I knew I could handle the level of hiking in the backcountry. I didn't question Julie's abilities, although I wondered how we would mesh as hiking partners.

Much like Gretchen, Julie was outgoing, vibrant, and typically the life of the party. She mingled easily and hosted her friends and family frequently for dinner parties and barbecues... that is when she was home from one of her extensive business trips. She excelled at cooking a delicious array of food, and her home was exquisitely furnished. But more than anything else, Julie eclipsed nearly everyone in her ability to make a person feel welcomed and at home. I admired that quality in her tremendously, since I was not adept at or keen for throwing parties. However, Julie differed from Gretchen in a crucial way. She did not smear people the way Gretchen did, instead Julie built up people rather than tear them down.

Soon after the initial conversation, Julie left for several weeks. I researched various trails that traversed the Sierras and first considered starting at Horseshoe Meadows south of Mount Langley and hiking west into Sequoia National Park. The Cottonwood Lakes were an annual trip for me, and I knew Army Pass and New Army Pass well. These key passes lead into the western Sierras.

I even considered a part of the John Muir Trail, which is 211 miles of trail that takes you through the most stunning jewels of the Sierras: Yosemite National Park, Kings Canyon, Sequoia National Park, the Ansel Adams Wilderness area, and the John Muir Wilderness area. While I knew the entire trail was not an option, a smaller leg of the trail would give us plenty of incredible beauty and hiking.

I settled on the High Sierra Trail, which contains just as many stunning vistas and the best the Sierras can offer: massive mountains, craggy granite peaks, sharp ridges slicing through the horizon, icy alpine lakes, lush alpine meadows, imposing waterfalls, verdant forests, and prolific wildlife. The trail crosses 72 miles, which most hikers easily finish in under a week.

Since I could not consult with Julie, I waited to finalize the trail plan. We needed to discuss transportation. If we truly traversed the mountain range, we would need to get back to our car somehow going from the western side and back to the eastern range.

She returned home several weeks later, late at night. A week passed before I saw her at home because of our schedules. She and Bob were enjoying dinner when I got home from work, and their friend and colleague, Michelle had joined them. Michelle worked for the same organization as Julie and Bob.

"Oh, Wendy, so glad you're here," said Julie. "We are finishing our plans for hiking in the Sierras while the floors are being refinished. We are going up to Mammoth and hike to Thousand Island Lake and back. Bob and Michelle are coming too, so I guess that means I'm in charge of the trip now."

This news surprised me, but I truly liked both Bob and Michelle. Plus, this development meant I no longer had to solve the problem of returning to a car parked on the other side of a mountain range. However, much like my ski trip with Bill and his WWII buddies, the arrangement made me a bit of a fifth wheel. Julie, Bob, and Michelle had been great friends and colleagues for years. I had known them only for a short while.

"We're going to stay in the condo in Mammoth the first night. Then we'll hike half-way and camp. The next day, we can take a day hike to the lake. We'll camp one more night and hike out the next day. To make it easier, I hired a team of pack mules out of Agnew Meadows," Julie said.

She was exuberant as always. She had such an effortless way of adding fun and joy to any event, a characteristic I lacked at the time due to the enormous stress I had in my life.

With a team of pack mules to carry the gear, we all planned on bringing a few items typically considered luxuries when in the outback. I filled my backpack with a few extras like a bottle of wine, two extra thinsulate pads for more comfortable sleeping on the ground, an extra blanket, and a pillow. It felt more like car camping than backpacking in the wilderness.

On the morning of departure, I took my cat to the vet for boarding. Then I hurried home to hop into the car with Julie, Bob, and Michelle. We traveled the same route that I had taken with Bill and his WWII buddies to ski in January. In fact, the condo we rented for this hiking trip was in the same complex in which we stayed for the ski trip.

Early the next morning, we gathered our gear and drove to Agnew Meadows, where the Tanner family has operated its pack station, along with Reds Meadows Pack Station, since 1934. The rustic buildings provided an authentic historic ambience to the meadows and trail heads that lead you to crystal streams, arctic blue lakes, and rich forests.

The stables and corrals held several dozen mules, all of whom wore expressions that said they knew more than any human could possibly know about the area. Those mules had intelligence and insight. I was certain the group leader could have simply opened the door to the corral, and the mules would get the humans into order and lead the way.

With our gear carried by the pack mules, we took great pleasure in immersing ourselves in the beauty of the terrain. I had been worried about Michelle's ability to hike any distance even without weight, but she did fine on the way albeit at a slow pace. We took High Trail, which starts out of Agnew Meadows at 8,340 feet and ascends to over 9,700 feet at which it crosses the northeast side of the canyon with the Middle Fork of the San Joaquin River. The trail descends slightly to 9.400 feet before beginning another ascent to approach Thousand Island Lake at 9,840 feet.

Most people who visit this area regard Thousand Island Lake as the most spectacular of the alpine lakes in the Eastern Sierras, and I agreed. Banner Peak and Mount Ritter tower above the lake's western shore with their summits above 12,000 if not 13,000 feet. The lake has many small islands, although not a thousand of them, and the Pacific Crest Trail and the John Muir Trail both pass Thousand Island Lake, so hikers have multiple options for scenic routes.

The trail crossed a log bridge behind the pack station. Then it continued uphill through the pine forest as it led to switchbacks along a bush-covered slope. Close to the bottom of the switchbacks, we passed a trail sign that marks the boundary of the Ansel Adams Wilderness area, which runs approximately 0.5 miles from the trailhead. As we hiked up the switchbacks, the trail began to rise above the tree line. At the top, we had stunning views of the canyon to the west.

Once past the switchbacks, High Trail ascends gradually northwest on the side of the canyon. through verdant meadows, small streams, and once out of the pines, slopes of fragrant mountain sage. We could see the imposing high peaks of the Minarets, Banner Peak, and Mount Ritter. We also passed through small groupings of quaking aspens which bordered riparian areas. The views were breathtaking as we continued northwest across the canyon.

The trail was a total of about 15 miles to the lake, but we stopped a little more than halfway to camp by the stream fed by Thousand Island Lake and its sister lakes, Garnet Lake, Ruby Lake, and Emerald Lake. We came up to the clearing in mid-afternoon. For years, campers have stopped for an overnight at that spot. It had several well-worn patches of earth to pitch our tents.

The pack leader helped unload the mules on the trail, and we carried our gear in several hundred yards to the campsite. Before he left to return to Agnew Meadows, he told us to be careful.

"We've had multiple reports of an active bear up here. If you didn't bring bear canisters, be sure to hang your food and trash up high from a tree limb. Make sure it's high enough that the bear can't reach it," he warned us.

Then he turned his pack around, or rather those smart mules turned him around, and he followed them down the trail.

As always, I expected a trip into the Sierras to provide me with peace and inner tranquility. The hike in had been truly pleasurable, especially since I had no weight on my back. Already I felt the stress melting away as I found a flat area just the right size for my tent, and the spot was quite a distance from the others. I positioned the tarp, then set up my tent and secured it with stakes. I rolled out the thinsulate pads and laid the sleeping bag on top. Then I set up my MSR pocket rocket stove on a nearby boulder, pulled out a snack and sat facing downstream using the boulder as a back rest.

Bob and Julie pitched their tents closer to the stream. Then they helped Michelle pitch hers close to a grouping of small boulders, which would become the area for cooking and eating.

I opened the wine I had brought along and poured a glass. As I rested and breathed in the deep fragrance of the pines, I absorbed the quiet of the Sierras. Bob and Julie disappeared, but Michelle sat resting and taking in the scenery.

Soon, I heard what I thought was music. The notes were rising in volume, and I clearly recognized some pretty robust jazz. Out here? I got up to investigate. Julie and Bob were sitting on a ledge overlooking the waterfall, and next to them was a CD player. Julie was playing music in the wilderness. Personally, I prefer to listen to the water and wind, plus I would never bring such an extraneous item to weigh down my backpack. But we had the pack mules, so why not?

Still, the jazz jarred my nerves a bit. I wanted only the sounds of the wilderness, although I attributed my mild irritation with the music as evidence of my emotional state rather than Julie choosing her own way to enjoy the Sierras.

As the sun sank closer to the mountain tops, we turned our attention to dinner. I pulled out my dehydrated, foil packet meal and began to boil water. Julie and Michelle unpacked several pots and pans, dishes, wine glasses, and lots of food. Julie asked what I wanted for dinner, but Bob reminded her that I was "self-contained." Actually, I hadn't considered that we would cook and eat together, perhaps an old habit from my years of backpacking. I was eating my own meal when Julie asked me to come over. She held the tube and heating element to an expensive MSR WindBurner stove. She handed me the pieces and asked if I knew how to work it.

Suddenly, I was glad she and I hadn't traversed the Sierras together. She didn't know how to work her own equipment, and the stove was brand new. I set it up and lit it for her.

They started cooking, and their jovial spirits filled the woods with cheer and laughter. Their meal seemed to go in courses with salad first, more wine, cheese and crackers, an entree, and then dessert. They cranked up the music. By the time they had finished eating, seemingly dozens of dirty dishes and pots dotted their section of the campsite and the boulders.

I worried about that active bear with so much food and dirty dishes around.

The sun disappeared and nighttime approached quickly. I had a bear canister for my food, but they did not. I put the canister far away from the tents, just in case that active bear wanted to try to open it. Their food and trash went into plastic garbage bags, and Julie and Bob went off to hang the bags from a pine tree. Michelle washed the dishes after borrowing my Campsuds to do so. I got a little irritated when she returned the bottle nearly empty.

We sat and chatted by lantern light for a few hours before we all retired to our tents.

Once in my sleeping bag, I tried to focus on the beauty of the mountains, but I could not force the broken records in my brain to cease turning. Throughout that year, nighttime meant reliving the sexual harassment and sexual abuse. Nights brought questions, anguish, despair, insomnia, and nightmares when I finally fall asleep.

I had left off the rain fly from my tent, so I could watch the night sky through the netting at the top. The stars and moon moved through the sky as I tried to fall asleep. Suddenly, I heard a loud crash. I heard Bob unzip his tent as he got up to check what had happened.

"It's a bear!" he said firmly but quietly. "Stay in the tents."

That active bear came by to rummage for scraps. He managed to reach the bags hanging from the trees and rip them open without actually pulling them down. He spent at least thirty minutes eating what he could find. I could hear him rifling through cans and bottles as he snarfed up scraps.

Then I heard the most ghoulish, ghastly sound coming from that active bear. I had heard the throaty "growl" of a bear before while hiking through the Sierras, but this noise was an otherworldy, gagging retching noise that made my hair stand on end. Eventually it stopped, and I heard the bear take off.

In the morning, we all got up to investigate. That active bear left garbage strewn all over camp. It was a complete mess. Then we discovered a pile of what we surmised was bear vomit. Apparently, some of the garbage didn't sit well with that active bear's stomach.

Bob and Julie cleaned up the mess, put the food and garbage back into plastic trash bags, and rehung the bags much higher than before. I went back to my tent to reorganize. We left the tents and camp standing as we had only a day hike planned to visit Thousand Island Lake. I used a daypack to bring along water and some light snacks for the hike.

As I worked, I noticed Michelle sitting in the door of her tent with a mirror propped up on a rock. She was applying makeup…foundation, blush, lipstick, the complete look. This was a different type of trekking for me. Julie was rearranging her backpack and spending quite a bit of time with it.

Once all four of us were ready to hit the trail, I grabbed my daypack. Bob had a daypack, and I don't recall if Michelle had any pack at all, but if she did, it was light. However, Julie carried her full backpack, although the tent, pots, and stove remained at camp.

We reached the junction with the first trail leading to Clark Lake. Then High Trail takes a turn towards the west to lead to Thousand Island Lake. The saddle breaks over a picturesque meadow that frames the bottom of a highly photographed view—the lake with Banner Peak on the western horizon being reflected in the glasslike water below. It is a stunning, crystalline blue lake with wild islands beneath an epic mountain range. We hiked down the trail towards the north shore and found a tiny crescent shaped cove that made for a nice little alpine beach with an awe-inspiring view of Banner Peak.

I intended to take the path to circle the lake, something I had done many years before. Although the lake is hugely popular with hikers and campers, we appeared to be the solitary visitors that day. Michelle looked tired. In fact, the entire hike was clearly out of her league, and the altitude was getting to her. Bob decided to explore within a smaller radius from the alpine beach.

Julie took off her backpack and began to remove items from deep within it. She was laughing and being her usual ebullient self.

"Look what I brought!" she exclaimed.

At first, I couldn't make out what came out of her backpack. The items appeared crumpled and brightly colored. Then she produced an air pump.

"They're rafts! We're going floating on the lake."

Indeed, she had brought along pool floaties including a multi-colored beach ball. Then she pulled out pre-mixed, foil packet margaritas and several margarita glasses.

I loved Julie, and I admired her immensely. Still at that moment, her desire to create high-spirited, high-altitude merriment along the shores of Thousand Island Lake collided with my deep, anxiety-driven need for peace and serenity, which I always found in the high Sierras.

Somehow, I excused myself and started down the lakeside trail that circumnavigates the water's edge. About halfway to the western edge, I hiked north just a little way. A sloping granite hill offered a spectacular view of the terrain. In the distance, I could see Julie and Michelle floating on the lake on inflatable rafts and tossing the beach ball between them. Their margarita-fueled laughter carried through the area echoing against the granite walls.

I knew the region well, so I cut over a low ridge to head over to Garnet Lake. On my own and out in the breathtaking scenery, I was able to feel the tranquility of the mountains. I stopped by the lake and ate some lunch before heading back to meet up with the group.

I couldn't think of any way to express myself to Julie. I simply had to accept that this trip to the Sierras would not be one in which I could find some relief from the daily tensions that were rising exponentially. In fact, I linked that inability to express myself to Julie with my inability to express myself to Gretchen, although that topic was much more difficult. Plus, Gretchen had already shown very clearly that she would reject anything other than the highest praise for Konrad. However, as I enjoyed the splendid quietude around the lake, I finally accepted that I would never be able to address the issue with Gretchen. Still, I could no longer remain silent about the abuse regardless of her reactions.

I returned to Thousand Island Lake. Julie and Michelle had finished floating on the lake, and Julie began deflating the floaties. We packed up and headed down the trail to camp, arriving just in time to cook some dinner, hang the food and trash, and crash in our tents for the night.

I arose very early in the morning and made coffee for myself while waiting for the others to wake up. That active bear had not visited us again, so we had no mess to clean up. The morning light grew in brightness as the sun came up over the mountains. Soon, Bob and Julie got up and made coffee as well.

I broke down my tent, rolled it tightly, and slipped it and the poles and stakes into its stuff sack. I packed all my gear into my backpack leaving a couple of water bottles handy for the hike down the mountain.

Bob broke down their tent, and Michelle finally woke up and came out of her tent. Julie made a cup of coffee for her and then began to cook breakfast. Bob called over to her as he worked at packing up their gear.

"What time do the pack mules arrive?" he asked Julie.

"We just need to pack up and head out," she replied.

That didn't answer his question, so Bob asked again.

"No, what time do the pack mules arrive to carry out the gear?"

"Oh, we can carry our backpacks," she said.

Bob looked perplexed. I didn't understand what she was saying, and Michelle didn't appear to be paying attention. In fact, she had returned to her tent, propped up the mirror again, and began applying her makeup.

"Julie, the pack mules should be here this morning, right? What time did you arrange for them to come? If they arrive in the afternoon, it will be too late for us to hike back to Agnew Meadows," Bob asked her.

"I didn't make arrangements for the hike out. We can carry our own backpacks," she explained.

I couldn't believe my ears. She had hired the pack mules only one way. My backpack was heavy with extra items, but I could handle the extra weight. Julie was strong, but this trip was too much for Michelle even without a backpack. She was unable to carry anything. What she brought had been carried by the mules.

Confusion ensued. Julie had brought way too much to carry out. We began divvying up Michelle's items, her tent, clothes, and sundries. I took quite a bit of extra things, the CD player, empty wine bottles, trash, and loaded them into my backpack or strapped them to the outside with bungee cords. Julie took a good amount, and Bob put some into his pack.

I worried about the hike out. Much of the trail would be downhill, but not all of it. Michelle looked worn out even before we left.

We took off as a group, but soon Michelle fell way behind. Bob offered to go more slowly to stay with her, and Julie and I kept our regular pace. Still, I hiked more quickly than Julie, and we separated after about an hour on the trail.

My pack felt like it weighed 75 pounds. When I first put it on, I almost fell backwards from the weight, but put my foot out behind me for stability. My worry about Michelle and Bob turned into irritation with Julie. Who in their right mind hires pack mules only one way unless it's to pick up and carry out the gear...not carry in the gear? I struggled inwardly with my growing displeasure with Julie. Her way of enjoying the Sierras was certainly different than mine, which I could accept. However, her decision to hire the mules only to pack in seemed to be a negligent, dangerous decision.

Although the High Trail was well traveled and well worn, we were still in the outback. People get hurt and die often enough that precautions should always be taken. Luckily, we had our cell phones and reception seemed pretty good if an emergency occurred.

I was deep in my thoughts and concerns as I rounded a sharp corner on the trail. I stopped immediately as I confronted a bear sitting on the trail just a mere three feet from me. I almost ran right into her. The bear appeared quite young and not fully grown. However, she was clearly older than a cub. Although I was not an expert in bears, this one seemed to be a youth, perhaps equivalent to a young teenager or a tweener. Yes, this bear was a tweener.

I looked at her and she looked at me. She seemed to say to me, "I'm not that active bear who ate your garbage. I have better taste than that."

For a second time in my life, I was blessed with a visit from a spirit animal. According to the Indians, a bear symbolizes physical strength, courage, and leadership. It was a protector and a good omen. Some Indian tribes believed you could evoke power from a bear if one showed up in your dreams. This bear showed up in real life for me, an especially good omen. I would need that power to survive what the coyote had predicted for me—the high voltage, higher level of conscious clarity. And, that was soon to happen in August, just weeks away.

Several quiet moments passed as we stared at each other when suddenly a thought flashed through my mind.

Ditch the backpack!

Just as I began dropping the backpack off my shoulders, she stood up and walked about five feet off the trail. Then she turned to face me as she sat down. She seemed very calm. "Please, after you," she said.

I repositioned the pack on my back and continued down the trail. After a few moments, I glanced back quickly. She still sat on her spot as she watched me walk away. I didn't stop until I reached Agnew Meadows, where I waited for Julie to catch up.

She was about an hour behind me. I inquired if she had seen the bear, but no, she had not. After we set our packs down by the car, we ate some lunch while we waited for Bob and Michelle to arrive.

An hour passed, and we began to worry. Julie tried calling Bob's cell phone, but he didn't answer. Another hour passed, and now we were very concerned. Finally, Julie's phone rang. It was Bob, and from what Julie was saying to him, I could tell they were lost. They had come to a fork in the trail and turned right rather than continue straight ahead. This took them further down the mountain and most likely across the John Muir trail heading towards Ediza Lake. Both Bob and Michelle were so exhausted, they couldn't go any further. Bob couldn't carry his pack any longer. So, they stopped and called.

Julie tried to remain calm, but she was anxious. After some discussion with me about the situation, she suddenly began to head down the trail with nothing but her cell phone, which was getting low on battery.

"Where are you going?" I asked.

"I'm going to go get them," she replied in haste.

"No, you're not. Julie, what if you don't find them? You don't know where they are. It's getting late in the afternoon. What if you get lost, too? And you're going to go out there with only your cell phone? What if you do find them? Are you going to carry them on your back?"

She stopped, and we talked about the options. We searched around Agnew Meadows for anyone, but those smart mules were out and their staff with them. The pack station was deserted. Red's Meadow, also run by the Tanner family, was only about six miles away. They had pack mules and horses. Julie began calling Reds Meadows, but no one answered.

We didn't speak for quite a while. Some hikers came back to Agnew Meadows after being out for several days. They loaded their car with their gear and started off. As they drove by, I flagged them down. The driver rolled down his window.

"Would you do me a big favor? When you exit the park and go past the ranger station, would you give my cell phone number to the ranger and ask him to pass it on to SAR? Have SAR call me, so I have their number captured on my cell phone? Our two friends are lost on the trail, and we're not sure they can make it back before dark," I asked him.

He agreed, took my phone number, and drove off.

Julie was angry at me for doing that.

"This is not an emergency! They're not in trouble. Nothing is going to happen to them. Why would you notify the ranger? There's nothing wrong!" she exclaimed.

I ignored her. I prefer to be prepared, even overly prepared. And, yes, it could quickly develop into a situation in which Bob and Michelle would be spending the night lost in the wilderness with no food or shelter.

She called Reds Meadows once again and someone finally picked up the phone. She explained the situation and asked for help. They agreed to send over two men and five horses to go search for Bob and Michelle and bring them in.

"OK, that's good. $150 for that? Can you do any better on the price?" she asked.

I almost lost my composure. $150 for two men and five horses to find two lost people in the outback seemed like quite a good deal to me, but she dickered on the price. I was speechless. It was her irresponsibility that resulted in this emergency. Reds Meadows didn't budge on the price, so she gave them her credit card number over the phone.

About an hour later, a pickup truck and a horse trailer arrived. The two men from Reds Meadows unloaded the horses, four of which were saddled and one of which was equipped with tack to carry backpacks. We talked with them and consulted the maps as we tried to determine where Bob and Michelle had made the wrong turn.

The riders and horses left down the trail. Julie and I didn't talk to one another. I was tired and sat in a shady spot where I could see the trailhead.

A couple hours later, the riders and horses came back with Bob and Michelle. Everyone was relieved, and Julie was dancing around.

"See, it wasn't an emergency. Everyone is all right!"

We loaded everything into the car and drove back to the condo in Mammoth. An emergency had been averted, even if Julie denied the seriousness of the situation outwardly. The rest of the trip was uneventful. But I added a new entry to my collection of mountaineering rules: before trekking with others, first make sure they take safety seriously.

15

Indian Head Peak

I continued to experience considerable distress through the rest of summer. As many times as I made it up to the Sierras or out to the desert that year, the strenuous exercise failed to help me de-stress. Only riding Hollywood at the ranch in Baja had that effect on me.

While Werner and I typically headed to Baja nearly every weekend, towards the end of July, he invited me along on a trip with him and his nephew, Kellen, and David and his son, Adam. They were heading out to Anza Borrego to go pheasant hunting and camping at Palm Canyon. I was surprised at the timing. Summer in the desert is very hot with temperatures into the 90s and 100s. Still, I enjoyed Anza Borrego, and this was an opportunity for a pleasant weekend jaunt.

The pheasant hunt was "canned," and Werner and David used this as an opportunity to teach Kellen and Adam about hunting before heading into the Sierras to hunt deer. I hung back, not especially excited about this portion of the trip.

We then headed over to the campgrounds at Palm Canyon in Anza Borrego. It was still relatively early in the morning and cool. Werner suggested that he and I climb Indian Head Peak.

I had climbed Indian Head several times, and while it is long and steep in some areas, it is at most a foothill and not technically difficult. Just good hard work. I agreed.

I filled my water bottles, got my day pack ready, and headed towards Palm Canyon to take the trail west, and pick up the south ridge trail to the peak.

"Where are you going?" Werner said. "We're going up that ridge." He pointed straight ahead.

The ridge Werner referred to was the right ridge directly in front of the campground. The left ridge was the "Indian Head," although from the angle at the campsite, it was difficult to make out the head. The Indian looks up at the sky, and the first peak being his chin, the second peak behind the chin is his nose, and behind the nose, but not visible from the campground, is his forehead.

"I didn't know there was a trail up that ridge." I said.

"There isn't. Let's go" came the reply.

My thought processes were a bit fuzzy at that point in time, so I just followed along. The ridge was steep in some areas, but not bad. Just tough hiking.

Still, I was never the type of hiker who ventured off trail. Even when I was younger, I stayed on well-worn paths and always carried a map. And, I always followed my own rule of mountaineering. I checked, double checked, and triple checked my gear as well as the map. I always knew where I was and how I would get back to the car.

After about two hours of hiking, we reached the "peak" on that particular ridge. From the desert floor it appears that all a hiker has to do is go left, cross the bridge between the two main stems of the mountain, and scurry up the Indian's Head.

Not so. Once we reached the top, we discovered there is no direct, connecting route from the minor peak to the bridge. Behind the minor peak, the ridge drops significantly and veers to the right. Then, one must cross a ledge and climb up a dome in order to connect with the trail up to Indian Head Peak.

I approached the ledge. It was approximately 8 feet long, and at most 5 feet wide. The drop off to the left was at least 300 feet, and the drop off to the right was minimum, 500 feet. The dome was not a significant angle, but for my level of climbing, I would have had all the necessary pro. Instead, all I had were my approach shoes.

I stood frozen. I was terrified of slipping and falling. Werner was already at the top of the dome. He had climbed most of the major international class climbs in America, including Half Dome, El Capitan, and Tahquitz. This was a walk up for him.

"Don't look down, and just do it. Power through it. Don't stop your momentum when you get to the dome, just keep going," he said.

I took a deep breath and crossed the ledge. But I stopped when I reached the dome. I couldn't find a hand hold. Then I looked down.

"Stop it!!" he yelled at me. "Don't look down, look up. Look at me! Now don't worry about handholds. Stand up straight and walk up the dome. Trust your shoes."

Tears started falling down my face. I was frozen. I couldn't move. It was certain death. One false slip on the dome, and the only option was to fall at least 500 feet.

I don't recall anything else about the hike. But obviously I made it, because I am here today. I recall a little of the hike back through Palm Canyon. And I recall being angry with myself because I had not pitched my tent beforehand. It was dusk when we returned to the campground and I was beyond exhausted. I struggled with getting the tent up and secured. One shot of mezcal and I was out for the night.

That was the first of many upcoming experiences with my short-term memory blanking out for periods of time. The episodes were anxiety induced – terror induced and continued for almost 2 years. The terror of climbing the dome without the necessary pro triggered the first episode. I was soon to experience a greater trigger. Occasionally, the memories would return, as a remembrance of the remembering. But some never did. The memories of climbing up the dome to reach Indian Head Peak were gone forever.

16

Tell Us, Danielle- August 2002

Throughout that year, I had difficulties putting an end to the broken record in my brain. Now the broken record included the sexual abuse from my childhood. Still that summer, I didn't expect the distress to unexpectedly increase exponentially. My stress levels were so high, I didn't think it was possible for them to go higher. I was gone from the Navy and childhood was long in the past.

In addition to the sexual abuse scandal with the Catholic Church, other headlines made the front page in 2002. That year, San Diego was the site of national news. Little seven-year-old Danielle van Dam went missing from her home in Sabre Springs, a tony neighborhood in San Diego. She disappeared the night of February 1-2. The media picked up this story with wicked exuberance as Danielle's parents were purportedly swingers, and the media portrayed the two as negligent parents, a particularly cruel twist considering they had lost their young daughter in a horrible way.

Danielle was in second grade when she was snatched from her room on the night of February 1. Authorities conducted a massive search for her for close to a month. Investigators had a neighbor,

David Westerfield, in their crosshairs soon. His alibi for the time that weekend she disappeared didn't seem straightforward to them. He told the police that he had taken a solo 560-mile road trip in his motor home. However, investigators discovered strands of Danielle's hair in Westerfield's bed, laundry, and motorhome. They found drops of her blood on the floor of his motor home and on his jacket. Danielle's hair and finger and palm prints were found above the bed in the RV, and the blue and orange fibers found at the death scene were discovered on Westerfield's property.

Police arrested David Westerfield, on February 22. Searchers found Danielle's nude body in a remote area in the desert on February 27. Westerfield was charged with kidnapping and first-degree murder. Prosecutors brought Westerfield to trial very quickly.

The trial judge, William Mudd, allowed the proceedings to be broadcast over radio and TV, and the nation was transfixed throughout the 29-day trial that occurred across late June, July, and early August. A co-worker of mine had a small T.V. in the office that we shared, and he had it turned on to the trial during the entire summer. I had to listen to it all day long. Day after day, I listened to the testimony. I didn't want to listen, but I couldn't escape it. It was constantly in the background.

Although Westerfield was not charged with rape and Danielle's body was too decomposed to determine the cause of death or if she had been sexually assaulted, the prosecutor, Jeff Dusek, presented forensic evidence that she and the family dog had been in Westerfield's motor home. He insinuated rape.

The media continued to blare out the salacious details without regard for the family. They republished suggestions from the defense attorney, David Feldman, that the Van Dams had been leading a lifestyle of "sex, drugs, and rock & roll" that put their own daughter into stranger danger. Other stories from the prosecution side suggested that Danielle's mother had rebuffed Westerfield's advances at a bar the night of the kidnapping. Raping and killing Danielle was done in heinous retribution.

The prosecutors presented the jury with a profusion of physical evidence, which included fingerprints, hair, blood, and fibers to link Westerfield to Danielle's kidnapping and murder.

The defense pointed out that prosecutors had no evidence that linked Westerfield directly to kidnapping Danielle. They found no evidence that he had been in her home, and his DNA was not found on Danielle's body. Feldman played that point repeatedly, because prosecutors had charged Westerfield with the special circumstance of murder during a kidnapping. This allowed them to seek the death penalty under California law.

The trial took a grotesquely macabre turn when the focus became determining how long Danielle's dead body had been outside exposed to the elements. The prosecutor put several entomologists on the stand to testify when flies first began to lay eggs on the little girl's dead body. One testified that flies colonized her body almost immediately after death. One entomologist suggested that the first eggs had been laid in mid-February after police put Westerfield under surveillance. A third entomologist testified that the initial infestation occurred between February 12 and February 23. Yet, he admitted to the defense attorney that the "corpse wasn't typical" because very few maggots were found in Danielle's head.

The dueling entomologists painted a grisly picture of Danielle's corpse found in the desert, even suggesting that a blanket acting as a shroud over the body may have delayed infestation.

In addition, the police found violent child pornography on Westerfield's computer. Prosecutors used this evidence to show motive for the crime. According to the prosecution's expert on computers, investigators discovered 100,000 images on Westerfield's computers with 8,000 to 10,000 nude images. Eighty of those images met the legal definition of child pornography.

The pornography included some video clips which showed an underage girl being raped by one man as another man held her down. The prosecution played the clips, which included the audio sounds of the girl struggling against the rapist. Other media showing underage girls were displayed to the jury as well. This was all broadcast over media in real time. While the images were not displayed across public media, the audio was.

On August 6 during his closing arguments, Dusek, a highly skilled prosecutor, methodically and relentlessly painted an emotionally charged picture of a little girl being raped on the bed of the motor home before being murdered. He spoke directly to the deceased little girl, calling her by name and asking, "Talk to us, Danielle. Tell us, Danielle, tell us what happened to you. But you already have told us with your hair and blood."

In his efforts to secure the death penalty for David Westerfield, Dusek graphically depicted his version of the events that led to Danielle's death by tying together the forensic evidence of Danielle's hair and blood in Westerfield's motor home and Danielle's blood on Westerfield's jacket. Even though there was no way to determine if Westerfield sexually assaulted her, Dusek's tale continued to take the jury (and the watching public) through a step-by-step journey that sketched a definitive rape that took place on the bed of the motor home.

As Dusek questioned how Danielle's hair and palm print came to be on the wall above the bed, he pounded his fist three times on the railing of the jury box to mimic the sound of her head banging against the wall repeatedly as Westerfield raped her.

When he did this, I felt as if lightning had just ripped through me.

Adult victims of childhood sexual assault face another type of abuse when others question their memories of what happened. They endure accusations of false memories implanted through hypnosis or overly eager therapists. Their motivations are questioned. They face derision and dismissal as well as accusations of mental illness, delusions, and worse. Indeed, I already faced this treatment from Gretchen beginning earlier that year.

It doesn't help that rare cases do exist in which overzealous investigators manipulated young children into telling wild tales of surreal abuse. The McMartin Preschool case and the case against Dale Akiki represent prime examples of this. Both of these cases involved outrageous, bizarre claims of Satanic ritual sexual abuse that defied all rationality and for which not one shred of evidence was found.

In the McMartin Preschool case, the children claimed to have seen witches flying and taken through underground tunnels. However, extensive excavation of the preschool site failed to find any secret tunnels or chambers. From Wikipedia:

"There were claims of orgies at car washes and airports, and of children being flushed down toilets to secret rooms where they would be abused, then cleaned up and presented back to their parents. Some child interviewees talked of a game called 'naked movie star' and suggested they were forcibly photographed nude. During the trial, some of the children's testimony stated that the 'naked movie star' game was actually a rhyming taunt used to tease other children—'What you say is what you are, you're a naked movie star,'—and had nothing to do with having naked pictures taken."

Eventually, all charges against the McMartins were dropped.

Dale Akiki was treated equally badly. He had a rare genetic disorder that left him with an appearance that didn't show well on T.V. In his case, the children claimed he killed an elephant and a giraffe and drank human blood in their presence. He was ultimately acquitted. San Diego Public Defenders Kate Coyne and Susan Clemens deserved the award as California Public Defenders of the Year in 1994.

So, the issues about memories are important. However, what's more important is to listen closely to an alleged perpetrator's defenses. Usually, the perpetrator makes the first claim that the child victim is mentally ill, or worse, that she was the aggressor. Why else would she make up a malicious fairy tale about an upstanding, well-respected man? Some pedophiles believe that the victim seduced them. Their delusions reveal a very sick mind. Other victims who prefer to keep it a secret will gang up on the victim who speaks up.

Let me be clear on this point. I want to address the issue of memories. My memories of the abuse have always been in the forefront of my mind. I never forgot, nor were they "recovered" or planted in my head. I have never been hypnotized.

However, my body dialed down the amplitude of the emotions, feelings, physical pain, and psychic pain connected with the memories. They existed more as matter-of-fact memories that played in my head although not completely. I felt emotions but kept the nuclear-powered feelings at bay.

When Jeff Dusek pounded his fist on the railing of the jury box while painting the picture of little Danielle van Dam being raped on the bed of the motor home, those matter-of-fact memories became reconnected to the higher levels of pain. In a split second, all the emotions, agony, torment, fear, terror, horror, speechless dread, panic, and pain plugged into those memories, and the switch flipped on to maximum amplitude. My coyote in Oriflamme Canyon had predicted this moment—this high amplitude, high level of conscious clarity that brought the source of the pain into the sharpest focus.

I don't recall the rest of the day or how I got home from work. I do recall the psychic disruption and its effect on my work and personal life, which definitely suffered.

I couldn't escape. I couldn't escape the trial. I couldn't escape reliving the pain. As a child, I couldn't escape the sexual abuse. I couldn't escape the evil.

That split second opened the door for the flood of pain and emotions, and the Westerfield trial guaranteed the dam holding back most of the flood would burst apart never to be stopped up again. By the end of 2002, I was diagnosed with PTSD.

Just as more people die descending big mountains than climbing up, this descent from the metaphorical mountain crushed me almost to the ultimate consequence. Climbing Mount San Jacinto via Snow Creek earlier that year temporarily crushed me physically. But, the Westerfield trial nearly crushed my very soul. It took years of excruciating effort to climb back up the mountain.

Ultimately, I decided my agony regarding the sexual harassment was a proxy for the sexual abuse. Although I was able to physically escape my boss at the Navy, the anxiety followed me just like the gossip followed me. Gretchen's smear campaign was everywhere. The story of the Boston pedophile priests was everywhere. The Westerfield trial was everywhere. Like peeling the onion, layer upon layer of my internal defenses were stripped away that year as I learned the hard lesson of staying in the present while facing the pain of the past and embracing the truth.

Eventually, my boss at the Navy never suffered any consequences for what he did to me. Rather, he was promoted to a plum assignment in Europe.

However, on August 21, 2002, David Westerfield was found guilty of first-degree murder, kidnapping, and possession of child pornography. He was sentenced to death. On February 4, 2019, the

California State Supreme Court upheld the conviction and death sentence of Westerfield after the mandatory appeal of any death sentence.

On March 12, 2019, California Governor Gavin Newsom (D) suspended all executions against the will of the people of California. Although locked up for life, Westerfield will never face the final earthly punishment for his evil deeds.

17

My Dream Mountain

Two or three years ago, I packed my expedition backpack with supplies for a weeklong trip to the Sierras. I needed some solitude, and I needed to feel the joy and breathtaking inspiration that I find in the backcountry. I took off from Kennedy Meadows, or perhaps it was Horseshoe Meadows. No, maybe it was Lee Vining. I can't quite recall now. Anyway, I parked the car and paid the fee. Then I broke a cardinal rule. I chose not to register with the Ranger's office and file a trail plan with an estimated date of return. Come to think of it, perhaps it was at least twenty years ago. I wouldn't take that kind of risk anymore.

Anyway, I started hiking, and as always, I kept a fairly brisk pace. I had no predetermined plans, so I turned at trailheads that looked interesting. Soon I was just east of Sequoia Park, or perhaps it was north of Tuolumne, or maybe west of Mount Langley, yet I had reached an area of the Sierras that I had never seen.

Although it was August, the temperature was very cool, 40 to 45 degrees, and fog layered the moss-covered embankments surrounding me. Moss not only covered the floor, but it also hung down from the trees, and dew dripped from the ends. Repeatedly I crossed rushing creeks of icy water. I could not see the melting snow above because of the dank fog. Surely by August all the snow would have melted. I wondered if I had wandered too far north. Perhaps I had gone too far. Perhaps I was in Washington or Canada.

Anyway, I wasn't tired, so I continued to hike through the nights. Although the days were foggy, the nights were completely clear, and the full moon lit the way each night. Finally, on the fifth day I stopped around noon for a sip of water. I looked west and saw a switchback as steep as I have ever encountered. It led to a saddle between two peaks, although I could not see the peaks themselves. Just beyond the other side of the saddle, sunlight broke through the clouds.

I headed across the narrow valley and started up the switchbacks. Soon night fell, but again I wasn't tired, so I continued on in the moonlight. Morning came, then lunchtime. I hiked up the switchback a full 24 hours before reaching the saddle.

At the top I saw the most glorious vista imaginable. I saw vivid hues of greens below and blues above, with solid granite canyons slicing through the mountain range. A single peak rose at least 22 to 23 thousand feet directly in front of me, and I could see the easy trail going up a gently sloping ridge to the top. The peak was stunningly beautiful, not craggy or ill shaped as so many peaks are in the Sierras. Although the mountain was granite, it seemed to be a perfectly shaped volcano, symmetrical with a rounded top. The gradations of colors led from deep chocolate browns and cadmium greens to azurite blues and pearlescent whites.

That mountain had me hooked. I had to bag this peak and see the 360-degree view from the top. I pulled out my maps and tried to find it, but I could not find the mountain on any of them. Apparently, I was the first to discover it. I had discovered the highest mountain on the North American continent. I would be the first to climb it, and it appeared to be an easy climb. Well, the first to climb it since the Indians, because the trail up to the peak was obviously an ancient Indian trail. Of course, I would name the mountain after myself.

I sat down to eat some lunch, and as I did a voice in the wind whispered to me, "it's an ass kicker." I looked across the valley at the peak, and I heeded the voice in the wind.

"Yes," I said to myself, "it has to be an ass kicker. It's a pretty package, but this mountain could hurt me."

I enjoyed the view while I ate, then I packed up and headed out. By nightfall I was back at my car. I stopped at Gretchen's house unannounced on the drive home and had dinner with her. She set a beautiful table as usual with her wonderfully extensive collection of unique dishes from all over the world.

"How a dinner is presented is just the same as how a gift is wrapped," she said. I had heard this before. Usually, her obsession with appearances annoyed me. This time I asked her a question.

"But what if the dinner is tainted with e-coli, and it could kill you, what does it matter how it is presented?"

"Oh, who cares? What does it matter if it looks this exquisite on the plate? Who cares what's inside a present if the wrapping is beautiful?" she exclaimed.

I chose not to continue with that conversation, and I changed the subject to something more congenial.

As I headed home, I considered her comment. Perhaps some packages aren't meant to be unwrapped, just as some mountains aren't meant to be climbed.

18

Mother's Day at the Ritz Carlton

Although I saw Gretchen very irregularly after that Easter in 2002, typically only for a holiday, I did make plans with her for Mother's Day each year. After Dad passed away, I took her to Mother's Day brunch at the Ritz Carlton in Laguna Niguel for several years even after the fateful Easter. I made reservations for the upcoming day and let her know that I would pick her up at home around 10 a.m. so she could attend church first.

The Ritz Carlton serves an opulent Mother's Day brunch with a buffet of seemingly endless options. Shaved white truffles in your individually crafted omelet? Prime rib? Lobster? Crab? Cheese trays, exotic fruits, sumptuous chocolate pastries, champagne are abundant. It's expensive at $110 per person, but the menu is extensive with luxurious samplings you simply did not have every day or even once a year.

Gretchen always seemed to enjoy the experience, so I continued to take her back. However, this year something seemed different as soon as I arrived at her home. She was beautifully, tastefully dressed.

She was a meticulous housekeeper, and every item of decor was in place, polished, and clean at all times. Two bookshelves lined the entryway, and they were artfully filled with books on Jesus by popular contemporary authors: Billy Graham, Max Lucado, Chuck Colson, Chuck Swindoll, Rick Warren, among others. Her other bookshelves in the office were filled with cookbooks, all of which she had read from cover to cover.

The house and her all-white carpeting were spotless and in order. However, she didn't really invite me in first, which she would typically do. She would normally offer a cup of coffee or want to point out some newly acquired treasure. This time, she was ready to leave immediately. I couldn't shake the feeling that something seemed off, although I couldn't pinpoint the issue. For a while I thought perhaps I was the one feeling askew and mistakenly projecting those feelings onto the situation. Then I rejected that idea. I had long ago come to acceptance that Gretchen and I would never have a meeting of the minds about Konrad. I was willing to drop the subject and simply see her only occasionally.

Her greeting seemed superficial as well. I shrugged it off, determined to enjoy the brunch and the lovely atmosphere of the Ritz Carlton overlooking the beach. The conversation in the car was non-personal, mostly about the weather and the cost of water and electricity in California. Since she was on a fixed income, these issues were rightfully of considerable importance to her.

We arrived and left the car with the valet. The entrance into the lobby and grand hallway were exquisitely adorned with monumental floral displays. The grand hallway ended at the bar overlooking the ocean. Since we were about an hour early by plan, we stopped there for a glass of wine. Gretchen was always the more talkative of the two of us, and frequently I let her determine the direction of the conversation. This Mother's Day was no different. I was content to let her talk as I found that focusing my thoughts on the day proved to be difficult. Looking out over the ocean and this particular beach brought back memories of high school in Orange County. I frequented this beach with friends long before the hotel chain bought the property and built the resort. Those were good memories.

After our wine, we checked in for brunch. The maître d' took us to our table and soon a waiter came to pour champagne. Pam, Gretchen's friend from church and her mother, Marilee, were across the dining room at another table also enjoying brunch. Gretchen got up to greet them briefly at their table. When she came back, we headed to the brunch tables.

As we ate, the conversation soon turned to a recent family event. I had not attended, but quite a few relatives on the Koosmann side were there. Someone had passed away, or it was a milestone birthday party. I don't recall. However, I do recall my thoughts focusing sharply onto her words as Gretchen continued to talk.

"Ken told Konnie that if he didn't stop talking to me like that, he was going to knock Konnie's head off," she announced.

Ken and Konnie are her brothers, Konnie being just behind Gretchen, who is the oldest child, and Ken, who is the youngest of four children. She also has a sister, Karen, who is the second youngest.

The pronouncement left me perplexed. However, over the years, I had developed an opinion about Gretchen's pronouncements. They were tinged with how she believed the situation should have been addressed, how she would have answered or acted, and that her desired way was the only right way. Konnie must have said something that offended Gretchen, and Ken didn't respond the way she wanted. So, in retelling the event, she inserted her own unspoken actions or words waiting for either confirmation or disapproval from the listener.

I wasn't at that event or privy to the conversation, so I have no way of knowing if it was true that Ken made those comments to Konnie. However, it was true that Gretchen said so at brunch that day.

Ken and Gretchen were intensely close as the oldest and youngest siblings, and it was well recognized in the family that they were steadfastly loyal to each other. However, her relationship with her sister had been non-existent for decades, and Gretchen frequently labeled her sister as mentally ill as her excuse for not staying in touch. Her relationship with Konnie was almost non-existent as well, and I had heard her refer to him as mentally ill and needing "heavy antidepressants" on many occasions.

Still, the idea that Ken would threaten physical violence against his older brother was preposterous. I didn't believe it then, and I don't believe it now. I didn't respond.

Gretchen continued.

"Karen always gets upset when I try to talk to her. There's something wrong with her. She's impossible to talk to and she's mentally ill. She's been on heavy antipsychotics nearly her whole life. Ken said not to talk to her about my trips around the world."

I tried to read her facial expression, but I had never seen her like this. Her body had become rigid, and she didn't look at me as she spoke. Instead, she looked out the window at the ocean. Her face appeared quite strained. It occurred to me that perhaps Ken hadn't even been present when Konnie spoke to Gretchen at the event. Still, the juxtaposition of her comments, first anger at Konnie's observations, then criticism about Karen, suggested to me that Konnie had denounced her lack of relationship with her sister. She wanted me to confirm that Ken, there or not, should have knocked Konnie's head off.

After a moment, I responded.

"I'm sure you don't mean it, but is it possible that when you talk to Karen about your trips, she misinterprets it that you think you are superior to her? Not everyone can take the trips you take."

Her expression flinched just ever so slightly. Then she froze and did not reply. After a moment, she stood up and excused herself to the restroom. I saw her return to the dining room after about twenty minutes, and she went across the room to talk to Pam and Marilee. It was at least another fifteen minutes before she came back to our table. She was overly composed, but her eyes were slightly red from tears.

Obviously, I had hit a raw nerve. Konnie must have made some apt remarks about her decades old lack of comity with her sister, and I just added confirmation to those observations rather that support her fantasy version.

The waiter kept Gretchen's champagne glass full, although I declined any myself since I was driving. The conversation turned back to the weather and the high cost of water and electricity among other superficial topics.

I considered Gretchen's response and her red eyes as we ate. Her focus on looks rather than substance could at times seem like a fixation on superiority. Her home was perfectly, beautifully furnished with expensive items from all over the world, items that she purchased on her many trips to many countries. She loved taking guests on lengthy tours of her home to point out her acquisitions.

I decided I was right. Konnie must have criticized Gretchen at this particular family get together about her non-existent relationship with Karen. Perhaps, she responded with her usual accusations of mental illness in the other person to explain her own choices. She was doing that right then at the table. Again, Gretchen has many fine qualities. We all do. At the same time, we all have areas in our lives that need work. This is the danger of Sola Fide. It's tempting for some people to ignore confession and repentance with the knowledge that faith alone gets you into heaven. Deflecting and blaming are responses that I have seen Gretchen proffer many times when confronted with less than perfect aspects of her character.

That was the moment in which I reached my limit with Gretchen's continuing smear campaign against me. Apparently, she was still unaware that so many family and friends were telling me what she was saying about me. In our family, honoring your father and mother is expected, demanded. That Commandment was never to be violated. However, I could no longer stand being around her. She wasn't acting as a mother should. She was a backstabber, a traitor, a Judas. She sold me out to cover her own shortcomings as a mother. She sold me down the river to deflect her own failings and to maintain her all-consuming preoccupation with the manufactured pretense of being a perfect mother. She threw me under the bus, tossed me to the wolves, had me tarred and feathered, drawn and quartered, and ridden out of town on a rail all at the same time.

She did nothing to protect me as a child. She protected her pedophile father and her own appearances. The truly bizarre element to her smears was the nature of the slander. By telling people that some unnamed, mythical doctor who has never met me diagnosed me with borderline personality disorder, she was drawing attention to her own failures as a mother. The etiology of the disorder involves extreme abuse and neglect to a child.

I couldn't understand myself; why I would take her to such a luxurious Mother's Day brunch knowing what I knew? Why would I even recognize Mother's Day? I was angry with myself and her. She didn't deserve to be honored, even if the Bible demands it. What about honoring your child?

I wanted to scream it all out loud. However, I already knew from my experience in Nepal that doing so gave her the excuse for denial.

I knew from Easter that talking about pedophile priests gave her the impetus to launch her war against me.

And, we were sitting in the middle of the formal dining room at the Ritz Carlton. The Ritz Carlton was hardly the place to make a scene, and I'm not the type to create a disturbance regardless of the issue. The scene in Nepal was the aberration for me. I remained quiet, unwilling to confront, but determined that this was in fact the last time I would ever see her.

Sitting in the elegant dining room of the Ritz Carlton, I decided on that Mother's Day that I could take no more from her. However, I also decided not to speak out against her. I would simply stay away and confide in only a few trusted, loyal family members and friends.

I paid the bill and drove Gretchen home.

19

The Gay Priest

I wasn't ready to get back into my car and make the two-hour drive home to San Diego, so I came in for a cup of coffee and read the Sunday paper. Both Gretchen and I sat at the dining room table to relax for a few moments before I was to take off. We were very quiet, and she was completely unaware of my true thoughts.

The paper ran a story on the front page of the second section about a Catholic priest in San Bernardino. In his early 40s, he had fallen in love with another man, his very first relationship. During one of his homilies at mass, he took the honest route and told his congregation about being gay and being in love for the first time ever. He announced that he could no longer perform his duties as a priest, so he resigned from the priesthood and the Roman Catholic Church. He went down the street, opened his own church, and about 90 percent of the congregation followed him.

The Catholic Church hierarchy was aghast. The article related their response to what they saw as an outrage. The Diocese convened an investigation and planned a form of church trial that hadn't been used in over 1,000 years. The ex-priest was laughing.

"What are they going to do? Fire me? I quit," the paper quoted him.

I recounted the story to Gretchen as we sipped our coffee. Then she suddenly made another pronouncement.

"All homosexuals are pedophiles," she said self-righteously and firmly.

I thought about this for a moment. She was wrong of course, but she was also from another generation.

For a fleeting moment, I wondered if this might be one last opportunity to open the subject of Konrad and sexual abuse. Her previous actions convinced me that she would deny the reality in a frantic effort to protect herself from the truth, but I could at least try and watch her reaction. I had already decided never to see her again, so anything I said then meant nothing. She brought up the subject of pedophiles, not I.

"I think you mean that the other way around: all pedophiles are homosexuals," I said. "Still, that's not right. The statistics show clearly that the vast majority of pedophiles are heterosexual…"

I hesitated before continuing.

"…and the vast majority of them prey on little girls in their own families."

She didn't look at me at all. She was facing forward towards the windows, so I was looking at her left profile. Several moments of silence passed. Then her head went up very slightly as she began to talk, but she seemed to be in her own head, not in the present.

"After my father was bishop, the bishop after him, Gaylerd Falde, was out visiting the churches in Arizona. He was arrested late in the night at a strip club in one of the back rooms. The church called a tribunal of 12 bishops and pastors, and my father was one of them. They voted 11 to 1 to forgive Dr. Falde and let him keep his job."

| 145 |

"My father was the only one to stand up for what was right. The only one! He voted to fire Dr. Falde. He told the others: 'No sexual deviants in the church! No sexual deviants in the church!'"

Aside from the day turning very strange, I recognized this speech pattern of Gretchen's. When she wanted to emphatically insist that her version was true and shut the other person down, she would repeat her phrase while raising her voice in volume.

And for the second time in my life, when she repeated Konrad's words, I heard not her voice, but Konrad's deep baritone come bellowing forth from her mouth.

After a few moments of silence during which she continued to stare at the windows straight ahead, I replied.

"I'm committed to truth."

She turned her head and glared at me saying nothing. Then, she got up and went to the living room. I could hear her rifling through drawers. I gathered the dirty coffee cups and newspaper to take them into the kitchen. Once there, I sat at the tiny kitchen table facing the window to finish the last sip of my coffee before leaving.

Gretchen came into the kitchen with a greeting card in her right hand. The paper was brightly colored and the front was a photograph of an iconic California oak tree standing alone on a hill with the sunset and the ocean horizon as its backdrop. She approached me and held out the card to show me the photo. She nearly stuck the card right into my face, and her expression showed a surreal defiance I had never seen in her before.

"Tom sent me this card after my father died. He said that this is how he always saw my father…as an oak tree. Tom said so. Tom said so. My father was the mighty oak of the family. He was the mighty oak of the family!"

She was nearly shouting at me. I thought Gretchen was on the verge of losing her mind. But, one thing was certain. She introduced the subject of pedophiles that day. In response, I made a broad comment about them. I didn't mention anyone or any circumstance in particular. Yet, her mind went immediately to Konrad and to his defense.

She stood there with her Koosmann Stance holding the card in my face. Then it became clear to me. No door would be opened that day to directly talk about Konrad as a child molester. No, she was baiting me. She was indirectly dancing around the subject to finally elicit my direct accusation that Konrad was a pedophile. I had called him an abuser in Nepal, but I had stopped short of calling him a sexual abuser. Now, she wanted me to say that Konrad was a child molester so she could call me a liar and mentally ill and order out of her home. It was her only defense. It was Konrad's defense that she repeated, a defense that had gone unchallenged for far too long.

In that moment, I understood my dream mountain. This was the mountain not to climb. This was the package not to unwrap, at least not fully. Not here, not now, not with Gretchen. It would happen another day in the future with other individuals. I already had enough confirmation that she knew her father was a pedophile. I didn't need to make the declaration. She already did.

Somehow, I stayed calm, although the tension grew.

"It's a nice picture of a tree," I replied quietly.

Many creative writers have come up with ways to describe silence. Pregnant silence, deafening silence, a void of noise, absence of sound, unmistakable sound, you could hear a pin drop.

But the silence that enveloped Gretchen's kitchen at that moment was different. It wafted up from the very depths of hell as Satan himself ceased his strivings, turned his head, and fixed his gaze on Gretchen in order to gauge her response.

I watched her intently as I wondered if she would continue to cling to the lie or take a first step into the light? Would she continue to parrot Konrad's defenses for the rest of her life? At that moment, I truly didn't care. All I saw was a woman who used lies and slander to try to intimidate me into silence.

She turned her head away from me and faced the window again. I was looking at her right profile and could clearly see the self-righteousness, the defiance, the self-certainty, and her desire to squash me, destroy me. She would do anything to protect her secret. I saw no loving mother in front of me at that moment.

The tone of her voice and her next words dripped with sanctimonious self-righteousness. She looked hostile, and her words flowed in a staccato cadence with first the words being pronounced with spaces of silence between them, and then the syllables becoming detached from each other as she repeated herself. The volume of her voice rose as well.

"My mother taught me, don't shame the family. Don't shame the family!"

She turned counterclockwise—with her back to me—and she marched out of the kitchen. Moments later I heard the door to her bedroom click shut.

That Mother's Day and every future Mother's Day were now concluded. I gathered my things to leave for a final time.

As difficult as the confrontation was, I left with a small bit of deep sadness and grief as well as anger. For the first time in my life, I had a glimpse of Gretchen as a child crying to her own mother, only to be rebuffed and relegated to a lifetime of shame, secrets, and silence.

Gretchen never learned the lesson. Victims don't shame the family; it's the perp who shames himself.

It took me many years to supplant the feelings of anger and loathing towards Gretchen. That brief glimpse of her as a little girl has mostly replaced any other picture of her, which made it possible to be a bit more empathetic. However, it was a difficult path to get to that point, and it is a difficult path that I will continue on over my entire life.

I learned an invaluable lesson that day. Truth is the sharpest weapon of all. Wielding truth must be done with great care and precise timing. When I hurled the truth out of pain and anguish at Gretchen in Nepal, I did nothing more than give her justification for denial. However, when I refused to be baited into speaking truth directly thereby refusing to fill the quiet void, it left no room for a denial from her. Then I heard the thoughts that filled her mind at that moment. I heard the words of her mother, Alice Kolpack Koosmann. Don't shame the family.

I also learned that my path to true inner peace began that day when I stood my ground. That was the day I completed taking back my own narrative, and I found a growing sense of inner tranquility.

I left that day and did not return for many years.

20

Epilogue

It wasn't until 2006, four years after the David Westerfield trial, that I returned to the mountains. A good climbing partner, Catherine, and I hiked up Mount San Jacinto using the Devil's Slide trail on the July 4th holiday. July 4th always holds special significance to me since it was my father's birthday. He had been gone for 8 years, and he was on my mind a lot that day.

We started up the switchbacks of Devil's Slide trail, which is the most difficult portion of the hike in my opinion. We took a quick break when we reached Saddle Junction. The trail to Tahquitz heads to the sharp right from the junction. You can go straight ahead and take a back route to Round Valley. But to summit Mount San Jacinto, we turned left towards Wellman's Divide.

A little more than halfway to Wellman's Divide, we passed the trail to Strawberry Creek towards the west. This part of the trail is wooded with fragrant pine trees. The shady trail typically remains quite a bit cooler than the higher sections of the path.

As we reached the end of the wooded area, we stepped into the sunlight. The path skirts across the east side of Marion Mountain through meadows that frequently have trickles of water draining down the mountain side and over the paths. This part of the trail has no pine trees for shade. Instead, it is covered with Manzanita and patches of skunk cabbage.

Catherine and I stepped into this sunny side of the trail. Within a few feet, we stopped short. A statuesque bald eagle stood still in the patch of skunk cabbage just about six feet from us. I should have grabbed my camera, but I didn't want the eagle to take off while I was distracted. This majestic bird was close to three feet tall, and it stood its ground despite our appearance. It clearly had no fear of humans, and its piercing eyes took in the sight of two hikers in an instant.

Even though Catherine was with me, I knew that this bald eagle was put in my path for a purpose. The visit by this regal inhabitant of the wilderness was my third time to be blessed with a spirit animal. Native Americans see the bald eagle as a sacred symbol. They are the highest-flying birds. Thus, they are considered to be closer to the Creator than humans or other animals. They symbolize wisdom, courage, and strength, and they are messengers to the Creator carrying prayers to the Great Spirit. In some tribes, eagle feathers were held during special council meetings to ensure that an individual would tell the truth. According to Indian legend, the bald eagle has the capacity to live in the realm of the spirit world while remaining in connection with Earth.

Perhaps in Indian legends, eagles only relay messages to the Creator. But on that day, this bald eagle landed and waited for me to turn the corner so he could relay a message to me—a message of courage, strength, and faith in the truth.

After a moment, that magnificent creature spread its massive wings, effortlessly caught the wind and took off in powerful, graceful flight. Catherine and I watched until we could no longer see his silhouette.

We continued on to Wellman's Divide. Eventually, the trail takes a sharp switchback turn to the left just before reaching the north edge of the mountain. This is where I had sat crushed, defeated by this mountain in 2002 while waiting for the other climbers to return from the summit after climbing Snow Creek.

I took the sharp left turn and nearly raced to the Mount San Jacinto Summit Trail. From there it was a short jaunt to the peak. Catherine and I found a spot at the top to eat lunch, and we tried to outdo each other with our gourmet lunches.

There at the summit, I went to the north edge and looked down Snow Creek. I thought of the long list of mountaineering rules I have heard, and none of them would have helped me reach the summit via Snow Creek. But that day, the mountain taught me there is only one true rule of mountaineering. All other so-called rules are merely extensions of it: respect the mountain.

That was 13 years ago. Now I no longer climb mountains.

Arthritis has set in my ankles and feet, which makes climbing difficult at times, but I do some nice, pretty hikes around San Diego still. Recently, my friend, Andrea, and I hiked up Mount Woodson to Potato Chip Rock, and we've hiked Iron Mountain as well. Compared to the 14,000' mountains I used to tackle in the Sierras, these are glorified foothills.

Eventually, Werner and I drifted apart. My emotional state made it impossible for me to be in a relationship at the time, although Werner remained a true friend for many, many years. I married in 2009 and had a son in my mid-40s. When he was about 3 ½ years old, I tried to repair my relationship with Gretchen, so my son could know his grandmother. We met a few times. She met my husband. She and I took my son to Disneyland several times. However, she fell into predictable ways, and one day took my husband aside to spread her smears once again. Then, she cut me off without warning. She made her final attempt to discredit me and no longer had reason to communicate.

I recognize more and more names in the obits now. WWII Bill passed away last year at the amazing age of 99. Werner passed away two years ago from Parkinson's and dementia at a very, very young 71. Julie is gone, and so is Señor Sandoval. When his memorial was held, his personal horse was set free ceremoniously on the ranch. John Havens has been gone for 17 years. My father passed away a very long 21 years ago.

However, as I write this, Ginny is still telling her stories of Winston Churchill. She is 101 years old, and she was recently featured in the local newspaper.

Even though I don't make it to the high Sierras much anymore, their beauty remains with me. I may be sitting alone in front of my computer or attempting to ignore the crushing din of rush hour traffic as I sit in my car. But my mind takes me back. I owe those peaks and alpine lakes plenty of peace and serenity to draw upon for tranquility in my later years.

I return to Thousand Island Lake in my mind frequently to ponder the mysteries of the world, to try to make sense of it. There on the shores, I wonder about Konrad and Martin Luther's revelation that salvation comes through faith alone. What is faith anyways? The Book of Hebrews tells us this:

"Faith is confidence in what we hope for and assurance about what we do not see." Hebrews 11:1

Konrad preached God's forgiveness and salvation through faith in Christ as Savior. He certainly professed faith verbally. Is that all it took for him to gain entrance into heaven? What about his actions on earth and the wake of devastation he left behind him? Did he have a deathbed confession? Did he ask for forgiveness? Can a pedophile even understand the depths of what he has done? Did his faith save him?

Sometimes as I visit Thousand Island Lake in my mind while I meditate and pray, I imagine that Jesus is waiting for me on the banks. However, he is not wearing the long flowing robes of ancient Israel. He always sports the correct clothing and gear for high altitude hiking. Then we walk around the lake and talk.

Every time my spirit animals, coyote, bear, and eagle are with me, and they follow along with eagle flying above. However, that sweet tweener bear is now a fully-grown mother bear always ready to take on any predator who might threaten her cub.

One time several years after the David Westerfield trial and my last Mother's Day with Gretchen, I asked him an impudent question.

"What about Konrad?" I asked. "Did he get into Heaven?"

He stopped and looked at me.

"Wendy, Wendy. What does the first paragraph of John say? You know it by heart."

"Yes, I know it by heart. It's poetry."

"In the beginning was the Word, and the Word was with God, and the Word was God. He was with God in the beginning. Through him all things were made; without him nothing was made that has been made. In him was life, and that life was the light of all mankind. The light shines in the darkness, and the darkness has not overcome it," I said.

"Yes," he replied. "In this world you will have troubles. Take heart! I have overcome the world."

"But, what does that mean?" I asked out of exasperation.

He turned towards the trail, and as he turned, he said, "Follow me."

Now as I hike the John Muir Trail or visit the Golden Trout Wilderness area or ski the slopes at Mammoth in my mind, I have learned to accept that I may never have the answer to my question, and that it is something that no human may ever understand. However, I have not accepted silence about the issue. Pedophilia and incest must be addressed in the open. Truth must be spoken out loud.

Even if I don't understand dueling church dogma like Sola Fide versus indulgences, I have gained an understanding of an important truth in my life. In the end, the person who dictated the overarching narrative was not Konrad Frederick Koosmann.

No, Alice Kolpack Koosmann, Bishop's wife and dutiful basement woman, determined the trajectory of generations of women for even decades after her death when she feared shaming the family.

Alice was from a different generation and from a different culture. Her culture gave us the Lutheran basement women slaving away in the bowels of the church as the men socialized above. Her culture put the priority on aprons, wooden spoons, and the appearance of perfection and righteousness, even if those characteristics didn't exist in reality.

What could she do? Women in her generation didn't get divorced or leave a husband. She would have been ostracized and shamed herself if she did. Women didn't have careers, although they certainly worked incredibly hard rearing their children, especially in farm country in the early 20th century.

Alice faced other challenges. What woman wants to accept that she married a child molester or a rapist? Who would have believed her? He was a Bishop. It wasn't until 2002 when The Boston Globe blew open the Catholic Church sex scandal that anyone would have believed it possible that a priest or pastor could be a child molester.

Alice would have been labeled delusional and severely mentally ill. She may have faced forced institutionalization in an insane asylum. Her husband would have had the power to do that to her.

In my opinion, this is where women's suffrage and feminism have had the most positive impact in enabling women to have careers and leave abusers if necessary. However, I fault the current feminist movement for enabling toxic feminism that demonizes all men. That element seems to garner the headlines far more than women who seek balance between the sexes.

The #metoo movement seems to have the resilience and power to correct this, yet the media feed on titillating headlines and click bait. And I fault women who allow abusers to manipulate and use them to do their own dirty work of discrediting a victim.

If we really want to create an environment in which pedophiles are stopped and put away before serious damage is done, I believe we need to focus the shame where it is due—not on the victim, but on the perpetrator.

Fathers and mothers, husbands and wives, brothers and sisters, men and women need to stand together against child molesters. We need to stop vilifying all men because of the misconduct of a few. We need to say, "We will not allow our children to be violated." We need to partner with the men and women who are not abusers and stand quietly firm in resolve even when the perp is a respected family member. We need to be willing to call law enforcement and follow through, not make excuses for the perpetrator. We need to say to a family member who sexually violates a child this:

"You are not family. We don't care what your position or relation is. Your actions mean that you are not family, and we will stand firm."

In addition, we need to speak truthfully. I read a book in 2003 called Miss America by Day by Marilyn Van Derbur. She was Miss

America in 1958, and her book revealed that her father had sexually violated her from the young age of eight until eighteen. He had been a respected member of his community and very wealthy. She recounted hearing her mother's footsteps ascending the staircase while her father was in her room molesting her, only to hear her mother stop halfway, turn around, and descend the staircase rather than stop what was happening in her daughter's bedroom. She also recounted how hard it was to accept that her mother hurt her far more than her father ever did.

The hardest truth I ever had to acknowledge was that my grandmother hurt me far more than my grandfather ever did. And she managed this even after she passed away when I was nine. Her legacy lives on through Gretchen. And Konrad's defenses live on through Gretchen as long as she repeats them.

"The little girl is mentally ill. Adopted children are defective. Pedophiles are all homosexuals. No sexual deviants in the church."

And as far as I can tell, Gretchen clings to the defenses even to the point of choosing not to know her grandson.

That is not my path. Taking back my own narrative began on a Nepalese plateau beneath the massive Annapurna range of the Himalayas the moment Aileen exclaimed, "Gretchen, that's child abuse."

Today, I no longer climb mountains. However, at some point in my life, I will climb my final mountain never to descend. Until that time, I will hike in the foothills and enjoy the view of the peaks above. I will enjoy watching my son grow, and I will always watch out for abusers in order to protect him. May he always be safe from predators.

May he always have faith in truth.

ACKNOWLEDGEMENTS

I have been blessed with many people in my life who have helped me through difficult times. I owe them all unending gratitude. They are:

Lola Hagan, Werner Landry, Julie Elliott, Bob Saunders, Bill and Ginny Davenport, Melissa Viets Burrell, Yasmin Ahmed, Neal Kline M.D., and all of my sisters in Christ at Community Bible Study.

I also owe thanks and gratitude to my launch team who encouraged me by linking my pre-order campaign on their Facebook page. They provided me with tremendous emotional support. They are:

Debra Lee, Kirby Olson, Andrea Cisneros, Ross Hill, Julia Montagnet, Karen Nichols, Tracy Tebo, Matt Tucker, Marcie Ward, Wendy Whitaker Morgan, and Karen Rittmuller.

I want to thank a woman whom I have never met, but admire tremendously, Marilyn Van Derbur. She was Miss America in 1958. In 2003, she published a book called Miss America by Day in which she revealed that her father, a prominent man in his community and very wealthy, sexually violated her from age 8 to 18. It was this book that encouraged me most to come forward.

ABOUT THE AUTHOR

Wendy Hoke is the author of The Bishop's Cross. She was the victim of child sexual abuse by her grandfather, Konrad Koosmann, who was a Bishop in the American Lutheran Church.

She has been a content curator, social media manager, and blogger for over 10 years. She provides her writing services independently, and you can contact her through her website, wendyhoke.com.

She began her writing career while working at a top 10 Wall Street investment banking firm, where she researched and penned a weekly, compliance-approved newsletter detailing the events of the tax-exempt securities market. Subsequently, she moved from Wall Street to Main Street as a senior manager for The Navy Exchange, a $2 billion retailer with operations across the globe including the U.S., Europe, Asia, and Iceland. After leaving her position as a civilian employee of the U.S. Navy, she briefly worked for the Marine Corps Exchange.

In addition, Wendy has been involved in her community by volunteering with Rady Children's Hospital Auxiliary raising money for social services for pediatric oncology patients. For 18 years, she participated in the Ocean Beach Community Dinners mission, which has fed the homeless for over 35 years.

She enjoys hiking, camping, golf, tennis, and cooking. Her faith is an integral part of her life, and she is an active member of a local Christian church.

www.ingramcontent.com/pod-product-compliance
Lightning Source LLC
LaVergne TN
LVHW012021060526
838201LV00061B/4398